MYTHING OUT ON JESUS AND HIS TEACHINGS

www.mythingoutonjesus.com

Embers Press Publishing

TABLE OF CONTENTS

INTRODUCTION

INTRODUCTION
HAVING EYES TO SEE & EARS TO HEAR

There is a universal truth in the marketplace: "Only 5% think, 15% think they think and 80% would rather die than think." We live and move in herds. We go along and rarely question what we hear. This is especially true after hearing things over and over throughout our lives. The tendency is to accept without question whatever we hear that is attached to a Scriptural verse and delivered by a pastor, teacher, guru, priest, imam, or monk we trust. I call these blind beliefs "myths" that are passed on so frequently that they become THE truth and a vital doctrine in our religious beliefs.

Once we have embraced a given myth, we tend to use it to establish that we are more right than another. There is something in our humanity that works overtime to be right, which makes those who disagree with us wrong.

I have been caught up in a series of myths my entire life. After growing up in a Christian home, attending a Christian liberal arts college and a four year graduate seminary, I went along with many of the myths without questioning what I read or was taught. The result? My eyes gradually glazed over and I became hard of hearing.

I've spent most of my life seeking to understand how to relate to the non-churched, non-Christian world. My books and speaking platforms have all had a crossover flavor to them and I finally ended up at the peak of professional speaking opportunities on the largest platforms in addition to pastoring one of the early mega-churches.

During that season of my life I came to the conclusion that only Jesus could transform our lives.

1. NOT Churchianity
2. NOT Christianity
3. NOT conversion methods
4. ONLY JESUS

I came to the conclusion that in order to reach the non-churched world I would have to separate myself from mainstream churches and Christianity. So, I did that to a certain degree, but I still had to take up offerings to keep the church and its staff alive.

In the second season of my life Jesus apprehended my heart in a fresh way and poised me toward taking this same "Jesus plus nothing" message beyond the "secular", non-churched world into the 7 major cultures of the world.

So, now my focus and perpendicular learning curve have taken me to a simple understanding of Jesus and the Kingdom. I've spent so much time and energy unlearning a lot of my theological premises I received at graduate seminary while a student and professor. It's been a fresh look at Jesus and His message of the good news of the Kingdom. His message was not the church, but all about the Kingdom. He only mentions "church" on two occasions.

In this journey now we are working with the 7 primary cultures of the world—Buddhist, Hindu, Moslem, Jewish, Animist, Christian and Atheist/Agnostic. We don't present Christianity to them, but Jesus. We teach them to follow the teachings and principles of Jesus as the early disciples did. The results are amazing. Instead of further dividing the world into more warring factions, we are experiencing a new and supernatural unity in the name of Jesus. You see, Jesus unites and all else divides! I am now convinced that Christianity isn't the way; Jesus is!

One of the repeated themes and challenges within the teachings of Jesus is to have ears to hear and eyes to see. Jesus knows our human tendency to drift away, get off-message, become distracted, and to divide up and take sides. So, He warns us to be careful that we listen and see clearly.

We are going to make our way through 32 myths. These aren't the only myths, but seem to be some of the most common ones. It is not my purpose to shake up your faith in any way other than to strengthen it and refocus it on Jesus. As you read through each of the myths, remove your religious blinders, think and evaluate what you believe Jesus' teaching really is. Don't be afraid to go with His teachings, when they counter things you have believed all your life. It may be a little shocking at first, but when the light bulb clicks on in your head and heart, you'll know what is true.

Jesus without religious baggage is awesome, attractive and even irresistible!

The only thing Jesus requires of you and me is to be interested — to have ears to hear and eyes to see.

If you are Muslim, know that your holy Qur'an teaches the uniqueness of Jesus and reveres Him most highly. If you are Buddhist, know that His Holiness, the Dalai Lama, loves the teachings of Jesus and encourages people to study them and follow Him. If you are Hindu, know that there are millions within your culture who have come to love and follow Jesus as did Ghandi. If you are Jewish, do as your many scholars are doing and study this Jewish Rabbi for yourself. If you are agnostic, you may be better able to check this out for yourself, who this Jesus without religious baggage really is.

If you are Christian, you may have the toughest time examining these myths. It's because you think you already know Jesus. What I have found to be true is that many Christians seem to know a lot about Jesus, but don't really know Him and follow Him.

Whether Muslim, Buddhist, Hindu, Jewish, agnostic or Christian, Jesus will never ask you to leave your culture. Jesus supersedes all culture. As a Buddhist friend said to me: "Jesus trumps everything!" If you myth out on Jesus, you will find that you are missing out on life at its fullest!

HOW ARE MYTHS DEVELOPED?

Now remember a myth is passed on so frequently that you blindly accept it as THE truth and it becomes a vital doctrine in your religious beliefs. Therefore it is, at best, a legend, a sort of spiritual fairy tale that has become a sacred belief for you and your community, yet it is really a well-intentioned falsehood or misunderstanding. For the most part, I don't think these myths we will examine were ever designed with evil purposes in mind. They have developed from one generation to another without questioning its veracity.

There is an old story that illustrates how myths originate and are passed on from generation to generation. It's about a family that always cut their turkey in half before they cooked it. This was certainly very odd by American tradition since everybody always served a whole baked turkey as the centerpiece for the Thanksgiving meal.

For many years this strange ritual went on until a child from the fourth generation decided he was going to find out why his family had such a very "strange" tradition. So he went up to his Momma and asked "why exactly do we cut the turkey across the middle whenever we cook one for Thanksgiving?"

Somewhat startled by such a sensible inquiry, the mother decided to ask her mom exactly the same question the youngest had put across: "Momma, Why 'do' we cut the turkey in half?"

Grandma for her part could only scratch her chin and reply, "to tell you the truth, I can't exactly tell why. All I know is that was how I saw my momma do it, and that's how I've done it all these years. Why don't we ask Great Grand Nanny!"

So they all huddled around the Matriarch as Grandma asked, Momma, why exactly do you always cut the thanksgiving turkey in half before you stick it in the oven?

Great Grandma sat her self up and with a look of disbelief she replied, "Did you never realize that our oven was never big enough to stick a whole turkey in? That's why I always had to cut those turkeys in two," Do you see how easily this happens? Now transfer this same understanding of myth development over to the world of spiritual things. Many times the myth emerges out of partial knowledge. You know there is nothing more dangerous than a person who has read only one book on a subject. From the basis of that book and that author opinions are formulated and become fact, until another person offers a different thought on the subject. I am reminded of the man who came to the conclusion about all native American Indians. He said, "All Indians walk single file, at least, the one I saw did." It's a partial perspective!

Myths also tend to be developed with a prejudiced perspective. Whereas a partial perspective is when you don't have all of the facts, the prejudiced perspective is when you don't want the facts. The facts might mess up what you already believe!

A man sat in front of his doctor, claiming that he knew that he was dead. The doctor assured him that he wasn't dead—depressed, maybe, but very much alive. Nothing would change the patient's mind on the issue. So, the doctor sent him on a research project to the medical library. The research would conclusively prove that "dead men don't bleed."

When the patient finished his research, he returned to see his doctor. The doctor asked, "What did the research say?" "Well," said the patient, "it is clear that the medical literature says that dead men don't bleed."

"Perfect!" replied the doctor. The doctor immediately went over to the patient, stuck a needle in his arm, and the man began to bleed. Without any hesitation the patient jumped up and proclaimed, "Dead men do bleed!" Now, that's a prejudiced perspective! Don't confuse me with the facts. My mind is already made up! Especially is this common within religious circles!

There is one other perspective that breeds myths. It's what I call a passive perspective. A passive perspective is when you have the facts, but don't act upon them. You are committed, but not involved in the behavior that the commitment requires. This is, by far, an epidemic in our society! Committed, but not involved! You know what to do in your marriage, but don't do it. You know what to do with your children, but don't do it. You know what to do in the midst of a conflict, but don't do it. You know what to do with your priorities, but you don't do it. It's like the kamikaze pilot who made 33 missions. He was committed, but not involved!

As we examine the person and teachings of Jesus we want to know as much as we can from Jesus, Himself. We want to examine Jesus and His teachings as objectively as possible. And, we want to examine Jesus and His teachings actively and not passively. This last approach can make the most difference. I don't want this examination of Jesus and His teachings to be just another intellectual exercise. It's one thing to know Jesus and His teachings and quite another thing altogether to do your best to follow Jesus: Follow Jesus because of His impeccable character and life. As you continue to follow Jesus, you will find His teachings to be most meaningful and fulfilling. And, if you embrace following Jesus as your lifestyle, you may discover how to relate to your Creator in a personal way.

DISCUSSION...

**What is it that most often keeps you from
having ears to hear and eyes to see?**

**Why do you think it is so easy to emphasize
so many things ahead of or instead of Jesus?**

Can you personally relate how myths are developed?

**In your opinion, how big is the problem
of "mything out" on Jesus?**

MYTH #1
JESUS IS OWNED BY CHRISTIANITY

Now don't get nervous about this myth. I am not bashing being a Christian or the religious system of Christianity. I want to help you consider a very basic understanding that causes lots of misunderstanding both in this country and in nations around the world. Let's examine it.

The definition of this myth is two-fold. First, this popular myth believes that Jesus was a Christian—that Jesus would be comfortable with being called a Christian and identifying exclusively with Christianity. Second, there seems to be a sub-myth on this one—that Christ was Jesus' last name. Let's quickly deal with this sub-myth. Jesus Christ is better understood as Jesus, the Christ. Jesus is His name and the Christ, the Messiah, the Anointed One, is His title.

The damage from this myth is many-fold.
FIRST—Christians believe they have a corner on the market with respect to Jesus. The by-product of believing Jesus is owned by Christianity is religious, pharisaical pride. This pride leads "Christians" to identify its culture as the right culture—the right way of life. This excludes all other cultures God created, other than the Christian culture, from following the path of God.

SECOND—If you desire to become a follower of Jesus, embracing this myth tends to distract you away from Jesus and the Kingdom. Instead of following Jesus, your focus can so easily become being a Christian or defending Christianity.

THIRD—Non-Christians believe Jesus is exclusively related to Christians and therefore they have no relationship with Him, even though Jesus is so attractive, irresistible and relevant to them.

FOURTH—Non-Christians identify Christianity with the disastrous and horrendous actions of its past—e.g. the Crusades against the Muslims and the persecution and killings of the Jews—all in the name of Christianity.

FIFTH—Non-Christians identify Christianity with the West and as they develop hate for the West, they develop hate for Christianity (and vice versa). When Christians attempt to convert people who are not Christians, they stir up such anger and hate—especially is this true in the non-Christian cultures of the world. Christians want Hindus, Buddhists, Jews, Muslims and whoever else is before them to become Christians—to be converted away from their cultures into Western Christianity. As my son-in-law said, "This is doing missionary work the hard way!" Instead of converting people away from their cultures and into Christianity, why not introduce them to Jesus and let Him do His work in their hearts. Now that's true conversion!

In debunking this myth I want to share four observations: FIRST—Jesus never used the term "Christian". The term is found three times in the New Testament. The first is in Acts 11:26:_**and when he found him, he brought him to Antioch. So for a whole year Barnabas and Saul met with the church and taught great numbers of people. The disciples were called Christians first at Antioch.** This seems to be a derisive comment by those in Antioch at this point. The second occurrence is in Acts 26:28:_**Then Agrippa said to Paul, "Do you think that in such a short time you can persuade me to be a Christian?"** The third time the term "Christian" is used is by Peter in I Peter 4:16: **However, if you suffer as a Christian, do not be ashamed, but praise God that you bear that name**.

When I use the argument that Jesus never used the term "Christian", I am saying that He had something so different in mind than to offer a label to be worn or an organization to join—all to be foisted upon the cultures of the world. If Jesus were trying to change people's cultural identification, He would have actually done so. When Jesus encountered a person from another culture with other gods and traditions, He was not concerned with "converting" them away from those backgrounds. He was primarily concerned with a person's relationship and trust in Him. Take the Roman official—the one Jesus said possessed more faith than any other person in all of Israel; Jesus didn't warn him to beware of the many Roman gods nor did He urge him to join the synagogue or any other organization.

SECOND—Jesus had a better term. Most Christians love to use the ID, "believer" or "born again". What's interesting is that with a couple of exceptions "believer", "believe" and "born again" are used only by John in his Gospel. John and all of the other Gospel writers—Matthew, Mark and Luke—use the same and most prominent terminology as they quote Jesus. All five Gospels are in agreement about the terms "follower" or "follow". This is Jesus' designation of those who are in relationship with Him—followers.

Without a doubt the best use of the term "Christian" is to be a "follower of the Christ". Used in this way following Jesus retains the power of a movement. However, most take Christianity as a religion, religious system of beliefs and an organization to be joined, which kills the movement by definition and practice.

THIRD—There is nothing wrong with being a Christian or even a Western Christian, if that's your cultural background. But there is something far better and that is to be a follower of Jesus. The largest spiritual movements in the world are happening among Animists in Africa, Buddhists and Hindus in Asia, Muslims and Jews in the Middle East, atheists and agnostics in China and even Christians in the USA. This movement numbers in the millions those who do not identify themselves with Christianity or Western Christianity, but sincerely and enthusiastically call themselves followers of Jesus. They love and worship Jesus!

How can this be? Because Jesus is more preeminent than we have let Him be. He is so much greater than any Christian can ever lift up and He must be lifted up. As He is lifted up Jesus will draw all men and women to Him, because He is the most attractive, the most irresistible and the most relevant ever. If the Creator-God were to ever take on flesh and become man, God would look like Jesus.

When Paul was in Athens (Acts 17:22-31), he stood up in the meeting of the Areopagus and said: **"People of Athens! I see that in every way you are very religious. For as I walked around and looked carefully at your objects of worship, I even found an altar with this inscription: TO AN UNKNOWN GOD. So you are ignorant of the very** thing you worship—and this is what I am going to proclaim to you. "The God who made the world and everything in it is the Lord of heaven and earth and does not live in temples built by hands. And he is not served by human hands, as if he needed anything. Rather, he himself gives everyone life and breath and everything else. From one man he made all the nations (cultures), that they should inhabit the whole earth; and he marked out their appointed times in history and the boundaries of their lands. God did this so that they would seek him and perhaps reach out for him and find him, though he is not far from any one of us. 'For in him we live and move and have our being.' As some of your own poets have said, 'We are his off-spring.'

"Therefore since we are God's offspring, we should not think that the divine being is like gold or silver or stone—an image made by human design and skill.** That divine being is Jesus and He must not be limited to the Christian box and culture. God set up all cultures in order for them to reach out for God and find Him.

No, Jesus is not owned by Christianity. He is the unique one, born of the Spirit of God! This Kingdom Manifesto of Jesus—the Good News—is for everyone. It is not exclusively for the Jews or the Christians. Jesus is all-inclusive. He is the ultimate answer for everyone everywhere. Jesus. Simply Jesus.

DISCUSSION...

How would you label your cultural background?

How does making Jesus an exclusive product of Christianity limit Jesus?

Where do you see the greatest danger in believing Jesus is owned by Christianity?

MYTH #2
BEING A BELIEVER IS ALL IT TAKES

Before getting into this myth I want to make it clear that I am well aware that many of you reading/listening to this series may not be Christians or from a Christian cultural background. The reason I feel I must examine several of these Christian terms is that I want to separate them from Jesus. So many of these terms are like barnacles on a ship and must be removed. Or, they are add-ons to Jesus that dilute who He is and what He intended.

Most of my life I have bought into the importance of being a believer or more specifically, a believer in Jesus. For years I have emphasized the term "believer" over "Christian", thinking this was the best identity to use that separates a person from the religious form of Christianity. If you perform a quick overview of the five Gospels (Matthew-Mark-Luke-John-Acts), you will discover that with few exceptions John is the only one who uses the term "believe" extensively.

The damage that is done by relying on being a believer is subtle, but lethal. FIRST—I have come to understand that this heavy emphasis upon being a "believer" is not sufficient to describe what Jesus wants from His disciples. Jesus demands more than this, as I'll demonstrate in a couple of minutes.

SECOND—Being a believer becomes a threshold experience—the very doorway into salvation—that Christians rely upon. After sharing a time of counseling a desperate man in the psych ward of a local hospital, I told this particular study group that it was so exciting to see this man's attitude of fear change into a sincere seeking for God. One of our group members quickly said, "So he became a believer?" In other words, "Did you close the spiritual deal and now this non-believer is a believer?" We seem to want this magical moment that a person becomes a believer and then all will be OK.

THIRD—Remembering the day you became a believer—your threshold experience of salvation—becomes a sure sign that your faith is genuine and not being able to nail down that date means that maybe you never actually have come into a salvation experience at all. This, too, can be a damaging experience. Recently, a pastor told one of his elders that if you can't identify that specific time of salvation faith in your life, then you are probably not a genuine believer. That night the elder interrogated his wife and she could not give him a specific day, but she felt she had come into a personal faith gradually. When the elder shared this experience with a group I was leading, he was really saddened by his discovery and it showed in his countenance.

Then I asked him, "When was Peter's specific day?" The elder sat there for quite some time and said, "I don't know." I said, "Troubling, isn't it?" "What about the other disciples? What was their specific day?" The elder saw what I was showing him and said, "So, my pastor was wrong."

The damage is done when we put such pressure on people to "make a decision" to be a believer in Jesus right now. This is why we ask people to come forward at altar calls and why we praise those who witness to the point that they have actually led someone to pray the sinner's prayer. It's all part of our instant approach to life. This wasn't the norm in the life and ministry of Jesus and it isn't the norm today!

FOURTH—To make "being a believer" so paramount, it is too easy to miss out on what happened with the early disciples and rely on man-made sound bites and clichés. Think about it! The early disciples were not "believers" in the sense that most think of it today. They were followers of Jesus and His teachings, but were a work in progress with respect to becoming believers. By the way, that process took them over three years!

To debunk this myth I want to offer some things to think about:
FIRST—Demons are said to be believers. In James 2:19 it says: **You believe that there is one God. Good! Even the demons believe that— and shudder.**

SECOND—The false teachers Jesus mentions are believers. In Matthew 7 Jesus refers to people who act like believers, but that's not good enough. Look at what Jesus says: **"Not everyone who says to me, 'Lord, Lord,' will enter the kingdom of heaven, but only those who do the will of my Father who is in heaven. Many will say to me on that day, 'Lord, Lord, did we not prophesy in your name and in your name drive out demons and in your name perform many miracles?' Then I will tell them plainly, 'I never knew you. Away from me, you evildoers!'**

Here was a group of people who spoke in the name of Jesus, cast out demons in the name of Jesus and performed many miracles in His name, yet Jesus didn't know them. He had no personal relationship with them.

THIRD—Many of you who are reading or listening to this daily see yourselves as believers, too. So, what's the difference? There must be more to it than just being a believer!

Jesus clarifies this. Jesus makes it clear that the only ones who will enter the Kingdom of heaven are those who do the will of the Father. And what does Jesus mean by this? In the next paragraph He illustrates what this means:

"Therefore everyone who hears these words of mine and puts them into practice is like a wise man who built his house on the rock. The rain came down, the streams rose, and the winds blew and beat against that house; yet it did not fall, because it had its foundation on the rock. But everyone who hears these words of mine and does not put them into practice is like a foolish man who built his house on sand. The rain came down, the streams rose, and the winds blew and beat against that house, and it fell with a great crash."

Those who do the will of the Father are those who hear the words of Jesus and practice them! That's more than just being a "believer". Don't get caught up in the Christian clichés and sound bites of religiosity. Pray for ears to hear and eyes to see, then listen to what Jesus says and do it. Don't miss this! You must believe, but you must believe enough to follow Jesus and His teachings! Whether you are Muslim, Hindu, Buddhist, Jew, Christian or agnostic, follow Jesus and enjoy the results!

DISCUSSION...

Why isn't enough to only believe?

What is the importance of belief in a person's relationship with God?

What does Jesus seem to add to "believe"?

MYTH #3
JESUS IS THE FOUNDER OF
THE CHRISTIAN CHURCH

This myth may be one of the most difficult to accept as a myth, but hear me out on it. Open up your hearts and minds and let's examine why I call this a myth. Remember, we're trying to understand the teachings and principles of Jesus, not the teachings and principles of our religious instruction and backgrounds. If I were to hold on to my background understandings, I would still believe Jesus was a Baptist!

Many people in the USA and lots more in the cultures of the world believe the myth that Jesus founded Christianity and the Christian Church. It's as if this was His intent and His purpose. This identification is a man-made connection between Jesus and Christianity and the organized Christian Church. When the Christian Church became an organization, Christianity became Christendom. The organized Church provides lots of services for the consumer, but it wasn't what Jesus intended. In Jesus' time there already was an organized Church in existence—the Synagogue. He didn't speak against it, but only against its leadership.

The damage of believing the myth that Jesus founded Christianity or the organized Christian Church is three-fold: FIRST—The religion of Christianity tends to become a substitute for the personal relationship with Jesus. Jesus commonly is left out of the Christian, religious, expression of faith. When I spoke at the major Dalai Lama event, those who were set up to represent Christianity didn't even mention Jesus one time.

One of my hobbies is to read over Christian newsletters and prayer letters to see if Jesus made the editorial cut. It is amazing how many times Jesus is left out of their expression of what their ministry really is. Just recently a major article was published in a secular magazine about a visible and prominent Christian leader and his plan to change the world. Sadly, Jesus never made it into any part of the plan nor did Jesus even receive honorable mention.

SECOND—The organized Christian Church tends to become a substitute for a personal relationship with Jesus and with His people. This produces spectators and not participators. It's just too easy to check off Church attendance as one of the things you feel you must do. But as powerful as the Church experience might be through authentic worship and exceptional messages, the once-a-week "show" just isn't what Jesus intended. They already had this experience in the Synagogue. There's nothing wrong with it; it's just not what Jesus came to found.

THIRD—When you believe Jesus is the founder of Christianity or the organized Christian Church, you expect Jesus to be the author and architect of what is done in the name of Christianity and by the local organized Christian Church. Therefore, Jesus gets the blame for it all! He gets tied to the Crusades. He gets tied to pastoral moral failure. He gets tied to the raising of money and endless fundraisers.

Now to debunk this myth: Jesus was a founder, all right, but not of the organized Christian Church or the religion of Christianity. Check out these observations:

1. Jesus must be separated from Christianity and the organized Christian Church. Remember the bumper sticker and later the movie: "Lord, please save us from your followers." To link Jesus with the organized Church or the religious system of Christianity caricaturizes Jesus beyond recognition. And then the world criticizes Jesus and His movement on earth based upon the Church and the religious system. This is as absurd as judging Beethoven by how well the local Junior High School band plays his music.

2. I have come to believe Jesus is the unique Son of God. For me to believe this myth limits Jesus in most every way. He is to be preeminent above all things, peoples and religious systems. To keep Jesus in the position of being the founder of Christianity keeps Jesus in His holy box and unavailable to the rest of the world.

3. Jesus never intended to found or launch a highly organized Church with membership requirements and man-made labels. He founded and

launched a movement—a dynamic, relational fellowship of followers of Jesus who love God and love their neighbors as themselves.

4. Jesus nor any of His disciples bashed the Synagogue of the day, which equates to the Church today. There was no thought or teaching on planting new Synagogues (Churches) to compete with the primary Synagogue in the city. This sets up the next observation:

5. The dynamic, relational movement Jesus launched was not about building an organization or a monument; He set in motion a movement that was loosely held together. This movement was not to take the place of the Synagogue nor is it to take the place of the organized Church today. However this movement is totally out of control—our control—and in the control of Jesus, the Head of His body.

It was to be a movement that orbited around the Synagogue (Church), the community and around the marketplace, demonstrating the love of Jesus to all. This movement doesn't have the privilege of gathering spectators together, because its all about participation in a fellowship, learning to love God and love one another. This movement is called the church (little c)—the gathering of the followers of Jesus into a fellowship. Jesus uses the term only three times, because His primary teaching was the Good News of the Kingdom. Big C Church was not taught nor was it in His mind or in the practice of the early disciples as they spread the message of Jesus and the Kingdom.

The book of Acts is sometimes called the Acts of the Apostles, but I think it's best to refer to it as the Acts of Jesus. The revolutionary movement of Jesus is still on today! The purpose of the movement is to do one of the most difficult things ever—to introduce Jesus to the world by demonstrating Jesus—walking, talking, thinking and loving like Jesus. You see, Jesus doesn't want you to demonstrate for Him, but to demonstrate Him and His love.

Jesus launched a revolutionary movement. Are you participating in this movement—the orbiting (little c) church movement Jesus founded— or are you still only playing spectator in a big C Church? You can do both and gain much out of your experience, but just don't miss out on the Jesus movement in your community right where you live! Jesus is already moving in the world around you. He's looking for you to join Him there!

ONE MORE THING: The Jesus movement that orbits around organized Church and the community is not made up of only Christians. The make-up of the Jesus movement is a vast variety of people from all kinds of cultural backgrounds. What holds this movement together is that each person, no matter his or her religious background, is a follower of Jesus.

DISCUSSION...
**Can you see how the religion of Christianity
tends to crowd Jesus out? How?**

Which is easier to follow—Christianity or Jesus? Why?

**Why is the religion of Christianity a turn-off to so many,
yet Jesus is ao attractive to most everyone?**

༄∾ P.S. #1 ∾
THE ORGANIZED CHURCH & THE JESUS MOVEMENT

Today and tomorrow I want to add two postscripts to Myth #3. I'm do-
ing this in order to promote as best I can that by lifting Jesus and the
Jesus movement up I am not in any way bashing the organized Church.
I am hoping these two postscripts will be helpful to do just that.

I want to clarify some of my thoughts on the organized Church today. I
know some of you no doubt feel that I am against the Church, but this
is not true. You see, I am striving to understand what Jesus intended
and what Jesus did, in fact, launch as the church of Jesus. Much of the
time we have added man-made doctrines and methods to His teachings.
These doctrines and methods may be good in themselves, but Jesus had
a better idea in mind. It's very important to say that I am not against the
organized Church, but seek to support it in its many ministries and to
encourage leaders and laymen alike to get back to the heart of Jesus as
they conduct their Church ministries.

When I teach what Jesus said and did with His disciples and what He
intended with respect to the future disciples of His disciples, it is clearly
different from what we know and love today in the Church. And as I
teach these things the contrasts are very clear, therefore it may seem
that I am blasting the Church in the process. That is not my heart at all.
I see the organized big C Church in much the same way as the early
Synagogues and the Temple in Jerusalem. When you frame the Church
in this way, it becomes clearer how the Church fits within the Jesus
movement.

The Synagogue and Temple were the mass meeting places where believers would come to pray, confess, offer sacrifices, worship and hear
the written Word of God read each week. The Synagogue had instruction for children through adults. Jesus and His disciples attended Synagogue, never spoke against it, didn't seek to change it, and didn't start
another one to compete with it. There just wasn't any bashing of the
Synagogue.

The Church today is the same as the Synagogue. It's a place where believers can gather in mass to pray, worship, hear teaching and enroll their children in some sort of spiritual instruction. It serves the consumer needs of the people. The mega churches provide programs that are unequaled and very helpful, especially to the needs of families.

The most vital question for today is "What kind of church did Jesus intend to launch on earth? What is the church Jesus said He was building?" If you study the history of the early church of Jesus, you will find that the church went in two distinct directions. The western orthodox, centering in Rome, were caught up in the litany of rules and regulations while the eastern orthodox, centering in Bagdad, were more into the person of Jesus. The west was more into establishing control, position and power, leaving monuments everywhere they went; the east was into fitting into the culture to make a difference, more like a movement.

So, the big C Church has its place in the plan of God, however it's too easy to miss what kind of thing Jesus intended. I call it the little c church. The term "church" is not a special or holy word as many believe and teach. It literally means "called out ones" and was used to describe city council meetings or any kind of assembly where people are called out to meet for a purpose. It simply is a gathering of followers of Jesus. The simple gathering of followers of Jesus on any day and at any location is a church. These gatherings Jesus launched revolved around four ingredients—fellowship, food, prayer and the apostles' teachings (teachings and principles of Jesus).

The big C Church by its very nature tends toward making most people spectators; the little c church is all about relational participation. The big C Church is founded on a set of beliefs or doctrines—a system of do's and don'ts; the little c church is founded completely on a personal relationship with Jesus and as we gather seeing Jesus show up. The big C Church is a place where you go; the little c church is not a place to go, but wherever you go you are to be the church—the gathering in the name and power of Jesus.

The big C Church is an organization; the little c church is a live organism—organic in every way.

FIRST—the church of Jesus is a movement. You cannot get your arms around it, visit it, or even see it. It's like the wind. You can't see the wind, but you can definitely see the effects of it. It's not a monument that one builds; it's a movement around Jesus that is contagious and must be caught. It's not a denominational or religious organization to be joined; it's a living movement through which Jesus captures your heart.

SECOND—the church of Jesus is everywhere and all around us—wherever followers of Jesus gather together in His name. No matter the location (coffee shop, living room, bar, race-track, battlefield, school, office), no matter the culture (Buddhist, Jewish, Muslim, Hindu, Christian and even agnostic), and no matter the level of society (the powerful or the poor), you can find the Jesus movement making a difference in His name.

THIRD—the church of Jesus is a relational, participatory dynamic where people encounter Jesus and walk with Him together. The Jesus movement is not driven by a certain doctrinal system; it's driven by a real, personal relationship with Jesus, Himself.

FOURTH—the church of Jesus is out of control—man's control—and under the leadership of Jesus, the Head. Maybe the one most deadly move we tend to make in life is to be "in control".

We are given a strong clue to what Jesus came to do in His prayer to the Father in John 17. He said, "Father, I have finished the work you gave me to do." Let's listen in own this prayer: "I have manifested Your name to the men whom You gave Me out of the world; they were Yours and You gave them to Me, and they have kept Your word. Now they have come to know that everything You have given Me is from You; for the words which You gave Me I have given to them; and they received them and truly understood that I came forth from You, and they believed that You sent Me. But now I come to You; and these things I speak in the world so that they may have My joy made full in themselves. I have given them Your word." Jesus came into this world to invest His life in a few men and now He sends us out to do the same. "As You sent Me into the world, I also have sent them into the world."

This is the essence of the church Jesus came to build—a movement consisting of a few followers who gather in His name in such a way that they are able to know the Father personally and intimately. He says, "I do not ask on behalf of these alone, but for those also who believe in Me through their word; that they may all be one; even as You, Father, are in Me and I in You, that they also may be in Us, so that the world may believe that You sent Me."

So, are you caught up in the dynamic, participatory movement of Jesus—being the church—or are you satisfied with being a spectator—going to church?

DISCUSSION...

How is the Synagogue of the 1st Century like the Church of today?

What are the differences between the organized Church (Synagogue) and the church of Jesus?

What did Jesus come to launch and what was it His early disciples actually launched?

⌯⌁ P.S. #2 ⌁⌯
THE MOVEMENT OF JESUS CAN FIT INTO
THE BIG C CHURCH

NOW before I begin, let me make it clear again: I am NOT against the organized Church. In our consumer-oriented world, the organized Church is the vehicle that can be a solution to the many community needs—to grow up as a family, to assist parents in strengthening the family, to provide a place of worship and prayer, to address the real needs of the community—hunger, clothing, housing and counseling.

Embracing Jesus' emphasis and intention with respect to the movement He was launching continually makes it seem that He was against the Synagogue (the modern-day organized Church). But this is not true. Jesus respected the Synagogue (the organized Church). However, Jesus came to launch a dynamic movement—a few here and a few over there, gathering together in His name. This is where He promised to show up—where two or three are gathered together.

And when Jesus shows up among the gathering of the few, He changes lives dramatically. This is a very critical thing. The church of Jesus is all about transformation. My friend, Bill Hybels, pastor of Willow Creek Community Church outside of Chicago, has probably trained more pastors and church leaders than any other. Within the last two years Bill and his staff came to the conclusion that all they had done building their church was sorely missing the mark. They found that their ministry had been emphasizing the wrong things—asking the wrong question, which was "How many people were in attendance?" The bottom-line is that the people were not experiencing transformation! They are now reworking their approach to ministry, identifying where each person is on his or her spiritual journey and ministering to their needs specifically. This was quite an admission, to say the least, and rocked the Christian world as the news spread.

My friend, Rick Warren, pastor of Saddleback Community Church in Orange County, California, shares a similar frustration. He shared with me his consternation over the glaring fact that the big C Church is just not changing the culture. Rick has been diligently training pastors as Hybels over the years and sees the reality that the big C Church is not having the Jesus movement impact on our society. Even though the mega Churches are more visible than ever, there are still 60-70 smaller churches closing each week. The net impact on our population is not increasing. It's like the big C Church in many ways has become a holy huddle in the midst of a troubled and lost world. But we cannot settle for this.

For the most part the leadership of the big C Churches sees the vital need to make the Church experience more intimate, so they break down the larger assembly into smaller contexts. One level of the smaller context is found through affinity groups—like couples with children or singles. Another level of the smaller context is an educational approach through offering a variety of classes. Then there are the smaller groups that meet in homes during the week to study a given topic. A final smaller context is more short-term, but proves to be quite effective and transformational—mission trips or retreats.

Any attempt to get smaller is better and creates an atmosphere that invites participation. But just because you are meeting in a smaller context doesn't mean you are practicing the Jesus movement. Most small groups never reach the level of intimacy and unity for which Jesus prayed. They usually drift into gentle friendships, which are good, but are not the revolutionary fellowship movement Jesus envisioned.

There are 3 dynamic, Greek words with a message of encouragement that can help you to stay on track with Jesus and to participate in A REVOLUTIONARY FELLOWSHIP THAT TRANSFORMS THE WORLD!

FIRST—parakoloutheo—Keep on recommitting yourself to follow closely after one another! It means "to follow close up, or side by side," "to accompany, to conform to", or "following" teaching so that you practice it. There is a sense of following so closely that you can more fully know a person or persons. (Check this out in Mark 16:17; Luke 1:3; I Timothy 4:6 and especially pay attention to II Timothy 3:10.)

SECOND—katartizo—Keep on restoring one another! In I Corinthians 1:10, Paul writes: "I appeal to you that you may be perfectly united in mind and thought." The words "perfectly united" are a translation of the Greek work, katartizo. It is used in several ways in the New Testament: to restore, to perfect, to fit, to prepare, etc. Possibly the most interesting use of the word is "to mend" a net. Fishermen around the world spend as much of their time mending nets as they do fishing. The maintenance of close relationships requires our attention to mending as well. It's even used for a physician to reset broken bones.

So, this word has 3 basic meanings:
(1) To mend or repair the nets—Matthew 4:21; Mark 1:19.
(2) To complete, furnish completely, to equip or to prepare—
      Luke 6:40.
(3) To prepare and perfect ethically and spiritually—I Thessalonians
      3:10; Galatians 6:1; Ephesians 4:12; II Timothy 3:17: I Peter 1:10.

THIRD—haplotes—Keep on reminding one another of the simplicity of Jesus! "But I am afraid that, as the serpent deceived Eve by his craftiness, your minds will be led astray from the simplicity and purity of devotion to Christ" (II Corinthians 11:3).   This is a fascinating word that has more to it than simply simple. This simplicity carries with it a sincerity, a single-mindedness, an unaffectedness. There is also a notion of generosity and bountifulness in this simplicity. In other words, the simplicity of devotion to Jesus has a single-minded abundance to it—an overflowing fullness and liberality about it.

As you can plainly see the church or gathering that Jesus intended has to do with experiencing a revolutionary fellowship with Jesus and those who are also following Him. Although this isn't the primary purpose of a week-end big C Church service due to the nature of its size, you can experience a revolutionary fellowship within the big C Church.

So, what does Jesus want us to do with the organized big C Church? Reading through the 5 gospels (Matthew-Mark-Luke-John-Acts) it is clear what Jesus and the disciples did with the "organized Church". Let's view the synagogue as the organized Church. There are four observations that seem most relevant to us:

1. You don't find Jesus or the disciples bashing the Synagogue (Church).
2. You find Jesus constantly correcting the leadership of the organized Synagogue (Church), teaching and practicing living in the Kingdom.
3. You don't find Jesus or the disciples starting new Synagogues (Churches), because of inadequate teaching or worship.
4. You find Jesus and the disciples using the Synagogues (Churches) and then orbiting around them.

Several years ago I read a book, ORBITING THE GIANT HAIRBALL...A Corporate Fool's Guide To Surviving With Grace by Gordon MacKenzie. MacKenzie worked at Hallmark Greeting Cards for 30 years in the creative department. He found that he was unable to be very creative, if he had to spend his time in corporate meetings. So he learned to orbit around the corporate bureaucracy and not be entangled in it, freeing him to create. He also makes it clear that the hairball was absolutely necessary. Without it there was nothing to power the orbit and the hairball paid the bills. This is exactly what the early fellowships of Jesus did. They participated in the Synagogue, yet they were in orbit around their Synagogue, their communities and around the marketplace. They went to Synagogue (Church) every Sabbath, yet they were there for a higher purpose. They were there to introduce more and more people to the revolutionary fellowship and person of Jesus.

There are two clear action steps here:

FIRST — participate in the revolutionary fellowship movement of Jesus inside or outside the big C Church.

SECOND — orbit around the big C Church, looking for those who are interested in Jesus and His movement. Once someone leans in with interest, invite them into the revolutionary fellowship of Jesus with you.

DISCUSSION...

Have you ever experienced a revolutionary fellowship of Jesus as described here?

What kinds of differences do you see between small groups and a revolutionary fellowship?

MYTH #4
JESUS WANTS THE ENTIRE WORLD TO BE CONVERTED TO CHRISTIANITY

I grew up believing not only that Jesus wanted the entire world to be converted to Christianity; I also believed my responsibility before God was to make everyone in my reach a Christian. That's just the way it was.

It was worse than that with much of the Baptist community around me. They not only believed Jesus wanted the world to be Christian, but Baptist. I remember sitting in a church service in my college town where a Baptist missionary made the statement: "There is no Gospel witness in the city of Cincinnati, Ohio." This shocked me, because I knew my uncle was a pastor there and I also knew several others. When I approached the speaker, he said: "There is no Baptist witness there." I quickly protested that my uncle and several other pastors I knew there were Baptist. He then clarified it for me: "They are not General Association Baptists." Do you get it? If people weren't becoming Baptists, then they were not hearing the Gospel message! This is just taking this thinking to its logical extreme and it is nuts!

Think about this myth for a second! Can you really believe that this Middle Eastern message of the Good News of Jesus and the Kingdom is owned by Western Christians and that all others around the world must become Christian in order to have eternal life? How haughty we are?

The greatest damage here in this myth is that Christians take on the attitude that they are the only ones who are right and therefore the only ones who will receive salvation from God. The secondary damage from this myth is that missionary organizations actually stir up more persecution than might have been. When missionaries insist on the natives "converting" to Christianity and to denounce their culture, they have the wrong goal. Of course, members of non-Christian cultures are threatened by this approach and react badly. What's worse is that they miss out on Jesus! Jesus is not the issue in those encounters; cultural conversion is!

I'm convinced that much of the persecution on the mission field is un-necessary. We are finding that when you make Jesus the issue and not religious conversion, there is an amazingly positive reception to Jesus. It's the same reception Jesus had among the non-Jewish encounters He had. Jesus is for the entire world. Jesus never urged anyone to become a part of a Christian culture or to join a Synagogue or Church. His only concern seems to be the person's heart of faith and the subsequent act of whether or not the person becomes a follower of Jesus.

Jesus made it a habit of reaching out to people from all kinds of religious and cultural backgrounds. NOTE just a few illustrations of how the ap-proach of Jesus and his disciples was all-inclusive: FIRST—In John 4, Jesus encountered the woman at the well. She was a Samaritan with very different beliefs regarding the center of worship. He left her with her cultural beliefs intact, except that He trumped the center of worship by saying that someday the center of worship will not be in a given location, but in your heart. Jesus was not promoting a new religion or defending the status quo; He was offering a personal relationship with God in the heart. This personal relationship would transform both her religion and the Hebrew religion. When Jesus conversed with the Sa-maritan woman, He didn't make certain to warn her of her false beliefs and be sure to change the mountain where she worshipped. There was no renunciation of her false doctrines. It was all about her relationship with Him.

SECOND—In Mark 7, the Syrophoenician woman was a gentile from a godless culture. Her faith was evident in her persistent conversation with Jesus about her daughter. Jesus honored her faith, however He didn't pull her into a new religious system or study class, nor did He have her renounce her cultural upbringing. The presence of Jesus will change a person from the inside out to be like Jesus. God's presence will convict their hearts in His time of what needs to be changed in their personal and cultural ways; NOT US!

THIRD—In Mark 6-7, NOTE Jesus' trip to Gennesaret. Do you notice how many times the Gospel writers refer to going to the other side of the Sea of Galilee? Whenever they were on the Jewish side, they crossed over to the other side. Why? Jesus performed the same works among the gentile world. He never urged them to change their religious culture, but let them remain right where they grew up. However, they were drawn to Him.

FOURTH—In Matthew 8, NOTE the Roman Centurion. No doubt the Roman Centurion grew up with the Roman gods, yet Jesus does not speak to this at all. His concern was his faith. When Jesus declared the Roman official's faith as outstanding, even greater than He had seen among the house of Israel, Jesus didn't tell this man to make sure to repent and go renounce the many Roman deities or his faith would be for naught. Further in the scene in the healing of the Roman Centurion's servant, Jesus says: **"I say to you that many will come from the east and the west and will take their places at the feast with Abraham, Isaac and Jacob in the kingdom of heaven."** Non-Jews or in our vernacular, non-Christians are going to be at the Kingdom feast. How can this be? It can only be through a personal relationship with Jesus.

FIFTH—In John 10, Jesus mentions "other sheep" that are His. Who are these other sheep? Could it be that they are from the various cultures of the world? Could they be those spoken of in Romans 2:14-15 and 1 John 4:7?

SIXTH—In Acts 15, the first followers of Jesus were all Jews. When the first gentiles (everyone else) came to Jesus, some religious Jews insisted that all followers of Jesus must become cultural Jews. The apostles clearly decided against this. All people could be followers of Jesus without changing their culture!

SEVENTH—In Acts 10, Peter's experience with the non-Jews is interesting and shocking to Peter. After Peter was supernaturally led to the house of Cornelius by a radical vision from God, he told them: **"I now realize how true it is that God does not show favoritism, but accepts men from every nation who fear him and do what is right."** Did you get that? God accepts men from every nation who fear him and do what is right.

EIGHTH—In Acts 17, Paul spoke in Athens: **"From one man he made all the nations, that they should inhabit the whole earth; and he marked out their appointed times in history and the boundaries of their lands. God did this so that they would seek him and perhaps reach out for him and find him, though he is not far from any one of us."** God made the nations—all nations; God made them in such a way so that all men might seek and find God.

NINTH—Also in Acts 17, when Paul spoke before the gentile audience in Athens, he didn't quote Scripture, didn't use Jesus' name at first, stroked them for their many idols of worship and proceeded to explain to them who this UNKNOWN GOD is that they commemorated. He didn't call for the renunciation of these "gods" and he used their "heathen" poems to explain what God is like (Acts 17:28), yet many believed in Jesus that day. What's that all about? I don't know many with this kind of approach.

TENTH—In Revelation 5:9, the reference is to every tribe and tongue and people and nation. Jesus came to reach all of these, not by exporting any given tribe, tongue, people or nation, but from within each of these faith in Jesus naturally emerges. Since the Creator-God is the source of all people, He has already marked all of these people groups. The word translated as "nations" is actually "ethnos" in the Greek. This is where we get the word "ethnic" from; in other words, there will be every cultural group who are followers of Jesus.

Anyone, anywhere can be a follower of Jesus—cultural Jews, Hindus, Buddhists, Animists, Agnostics, Moslems, and even Christians can all be followers of Jesus. Christians have said for years that a cultural Jew doesn't have to renounce being Jewish in order to follow Jesus. Following Jesus makes a person's Jewishness more full and meaningful. I believe this translates into the many cultures of the world. Following Jesus brings out the fullness of any and all cultures. A cultural Buddhist can be a follower of Jesus. A cultural Moslem can be a follower of Jesus. It's just like a cultural Catholic can be a follower of Jesus without renouncing his cultural background or a cultural Baptist or a cultural Methodist. Anyone can be a follower of Jesus and still remain within his or her cultural background.

Jesus doesn't want the entire world to be Christian; Jesus wants the entire world to follow Him. This is why Jesus gives us His primary command to carry on His ministry to the world. He says, "Make disciples of all nations!" Make followers of Jesus in all nations; don't try to make them Christians! Introduce them to Jesus.

DISCUSSION...

• **In your spiritual journey where have you drawn the line demarcating who is "in" with God and who is "out"?**

• **Can a person be converted into having a heart for God by debate and argument or persuasive conversation?**

• **How does conversion actually happen?**

MYTH #5
JESUS IS NARROW AND EXCLUSIVE

Whenever I share the message of Jesus plus nothing, most frequently I get an initial response—a quote from the mouth of Jesus: **"I am the way, the truth and the life...."** This usually comes from a person who is friendly to me and is appealing to me from what is considered to be a foundational statement from Jesus, Himself. And by the way, I couldn't agree more.

The damage that comes from seeing Jesus as narrow and exclusive fuels the sense of "we are the only ones who are right and going to heaven" and the rest of the world is wrong and going to hell. In addition to this, viewing Jesus as narrow and exclusive in this prideful way and believing that our way of thinking and believing is the only way, truth and life as well, does something that Jesus abhors. Embracing this myth shuts the door of the Kingdom on everyone else who is not one of us and we have become the judge on the matter.

Granted this statement of Jesus seems to be quite narrow and exclusive, but it's only narrow and exclusive if Jesus lives within the limitations of a Christian box. Since I separate Jesus from Christianity, deny that Jesus is the founder of the Christian Church and reject the mission of Jesus as being to convert the world to Christianity, people believe I must be removing Jesus from being the way, the truth and the life.
This couldn't be further from the truth! It's not that Jesus is so narrow and exclusive; Jesus is more preeminent than we have ever dreamed and He is all-inclusive. He'll work with anyone!

In Jesus' first seminar in Matthew 5-7 He made a radical statement with respect His relationship with the Jewish Law and traditions. He said, **"Do not think that I have come to abolish the Law or the Prophets; I have not come to abolish them but to fulfill them."**

Literally, Jesus didn't come to abolish the Laws and traditions of the

Jewish culture; He came to fill it full—to bring fullness to it. It's like the Jewish culture with its Law and traditions was like a glass—a form with some sort of structure to it. Then, Jesus came to fill up that form or glass to its fullest—to fill it full. Jesus came to bring ultimate meaning and fullness to the Jewish religious system. In other words, Jesus is the way, the truth and the life for the Jewish dreams and yearnings.

In the same way, I am coming to believe that Jesus is the way, the truth and the life for all cultural and religious systems and traditions. Jesus is the meaning and fullness everyone is looking for. Jesus fills up the various forms or glasses of every culture.

This may seem a little far-fetched for you to embrace at first, but give it some thought. We are finding the footprints of Jesus in every culture. Many years ago Don Richardson wrote a groundbreaking book Eternity In Their Hearts. His research demonstrated that the fingerprint of the Creator-God was found to be in many cultures. God is already there, because God placed *"eternity in their hearts"*.

In the movie, "Fingerprints of God in Japan", the Creator-God of the Japanese people is clearly revealed. In the past the Japanese people were told that they had to reject their Japanese roots and culture in order to be converted to Western Christianity. However, it is now clear that the Creator-God of the Japanese people was known to be in the form of a tri-unity or Godhead. Their Creator-God had a Japanese name, not the Jewish name of Jehovah. When the Japanese watch this film, they weep with great joy. They don't have to reject their culture; God created them and is already present there.

This same understanding has happened among the Hawaiians, Polynesians, Buddhists, Hindus and Chinese. What's interesting is that in many of these cultures there are similar stories in their history—the flood, sacrifices for sins and many have a garden scene. In several of these cultures their ancient scriptures speak of a sacrifice for their sins that must be made by God, Himself. Where did these come from? These are the fingerprints of God in the many cultures of the world.

Jesus is the ultimate fullness of the many cultures of the world. Hey, that's not narrow and exclusive; that's universal and all-inclusive. Jesus is the way, the truth and the life for anyone who has ears to hear and eyes to see. Our mission is not to plant mission stations in these cultures and teach them our favorite Western Christian hymns. Our tendency has been to introduce Jesus to a culture, stay there among them and orchestrate our Western Christian way of doing things. This methodology serves to bring the Jesus movement to a screeching halt in that culture.

Instead, our mission is to introduce Jesus to the cultures of the world and encourage them to respond with their unique, cultural customs. Most recently this was done in Hawaii and the church of Jesus is really growing there. Wherever this is done, the Jesus movement flourishes. Jesus is all-inclusive and wants to work with everyone.

DISCUSSION...

• **When the writer of Ecclesiastes relates that God has placed "eternity in their hearts", what do you think this means?**

• **Can you describe how narrow Jesus has been in your spiritual journey?**

• **Why do you think it's easier to keep Jesus in a Christian box?**

MYTH #6
YOU MUST BELIEVE JESUS IS THE SON OF GOD TO FOLLOW HIM

For years I've held this myth up as a standard for those who believe. This myth is so embedded within Christianity. This has become the benchmark for whether or not a person is a true believer.

The primary damage of this myth is that it has become a doctrinal standard or proof of doctrinal purity. If you don't believe Jesus is the Son of God, you are disqualified to even play the spiritual game.

By the way, one other point of damage is that when you embrace this myth that you cannot follow Jesus unless you believe He is the Son of God, you can so easily shut the door of the Kingdom to those who are interested.

Now, in debunking this myth I want to direct your attention again to the early disciples. When they first answered the call to follow Jesus, did they believe that Jesus was the Son of God? No!

They believed Jesus was the latest and greatest Rabbi on the religious scene. They believed Jesus was an amazing teacher and example. They believed He was able to perform miracles and heal people. They were highly responsive to Him, because He picked them out of a crowd and showed them some affirmation and attention. They weren't even very strong believers in Him at first either. They believed Jesus enough to attach their hopes to Him.

When you finally accept the fact that the early disciples weren't believers and didn't yet believe that Jesus was the Son of God, you step across a great threshold of truth. You see, there are lots of people that you know that are just where the disciples were in the beginning. They are curious, fascinated, impressed and interested in this Jesus. When I tell an interested agnostic that he is exactly like the early disciples of Jesus, he or she is taken back.

In Matthew 16, Jesus has a fascinating encounter and interchange with the disciples: **When Jesus came to the region of Caesarea Philippi, he asked his disciples, "Who do people say the Son of Man is?" They replied, "Some say John the Baptist; others say Elijah; and still others, Jeremiah or one of the prophets." "But what about you?" he asked. "Who do you say I am?" Simon Peter answered, "You are the Messiah, the Son of the living God."**

The disciples have been following this attractive, irresistible and relevant Jesus for quite some time and now the question comes from Jesus: **"Who do you say I am?" Peter's answer was right on when he said, "You are the Messiah, the Son of the living God."** This is the first time this has been expressed with a sense of conviction by the disciples. The thought was there, but this seems to nail it down. We believe Jesus is God's Messiah, the Son of the living God.

Now note Jesus' reply to Peter's answer. He first says, **"Blessed are you, Simon son of Jonah."** Jesus strokes Peter for expressing the right answer to the question. But before Peter gets too puffed up for coming up with this great answer, Jesus quickly says, **"This was not revealed to you by flesh and blood."** He is saying, "Peter, you didn't think this up on your own and no one taught you this truth." You see, we continue to rely on teaching our people a set of doctrines or beliefs, thinking this teaching will somehow be sufficient to establish and maintain a vital relationship with God.

Jesus goes on to explain, **"But by my Father in heaven"** revealed this to you. "Peter, my Father gave you this great insight that I am indeed the Son of God." This is still the plan of operation today. The Father transformed the hearts and minds of the disciples, because they have been following Jesus for a long time.

In II Timothy 2, Paul counsels Timothy: Those who oppose him he must gently instruct, in the hope that God will grant them repentance leading them to a knowledge of the truth, and that they will come to their senses and escape from the trap of the devil, who has taken them captive to do his will. Note that you don't get a heart for change or a transformation of heart and mind by any human methodology. Genuine transformation will only come as a gift from God—**"in the hope that God will grant them repentance leading them to a knowledge of the truth and that they will come to their senses."** God will grant this transformation to all who are interested enough to have ears to hear and eyes to see. It's a gift from God.

There seem to be three stages of following Jesus. FIRST—Jesus is followed because He is so flawless and attractive—unimpeachable. He is the one person who has truly walked the walk and the talk perfectly. No one argues with this. And the disciples believed in Him enough to follow Him. There is nothing wrong with this type of following Jesus at all.

SECOND—Then as you follow this attractive Jesus, you will begin to embrace His lifestyle, teachings and principles and find them to be very practical and meaningful for your life. Following this Jesus just makes sense.

THIRD—Finally, as you continue to follow this Jesus and find His teachings meaningful, you will at some point discover your Creator-God. You will experience transformation of your heart and your mind and see Jesus as the Son of God.

So, wherever you are in this continuum of the stages in following Jesus, ultimately you are seeking and hoping to receive this gift of transformation from God Himself. When you understand this, you then can embrace the fact of Buddhists, Hindus, Jews, Agnostics, Muslims and even Christians who are followers of Jesus.

This is why I have dedicated my life to doing two things. FIRST—I am doing one of the toughest things I've ever set out to do in my life; I'm trying to follow Jesus and embrace His teachings as my lifestyle. SECOND—I want to do whatever I can do to introduce Jesus and His teachings to as many individuals as I possibly can. This approach to life is summed up in an old phrase: TO KNOW JESUS AND TO MAKE HIM KNOWN. I encourage you to think about doing the same.

DISCUSSION...

• Have you ever shut the door of the Kingdom to others
  by requiring that people must believe Jesus is the
  Son of God before they can relate?

• Have you ever added any other pre-requisites
  before a person can follow Jesus?

• Why is it we have placed the early disciples on
  such a high level of spirituality?

MYTH #7
JESUS CAME TO TAKE ALL BELIEVERS OUT OF HERE

This is a prominent myth embraced by Christians and you may already believe I am heretical in my thinking, but hear me out on this. It will take two sessions to do it.

The damage with this myth is threefold: FIRST—We have so embraced this myth that we have become extremely focused on the sweet by and by rather than living in the nasty now and now. We have so embraced this myth that we tend to live in the tyranny of the urgent and plan our lives accordingly.

Jesus was all about Kingdom living being right here right now.

SECOND—We have so embraced this myth that we have wrapped our lives around the 2nd coming of Jesus as if we know when He will return. This seems to be a bit of a problem, since Jesus says that He doesn't even know.

THIRD—We have so embraced this myth that we are missing out on the most powerful proof of the love of Jesus and the presence of Jesus that bear witness to the world.

There are 5 basic movements throughout the bible where God is going in the direction from heaven to earth and not from earth to heaven. The first movement is illustrated in the Garden of Eden. The essence of God is relational and demonstrates the need for fellowship within the creation. God wants to walk in relationship with man. Check out what happened in the Garden of Eden. The first time we encounter lost people is in the Garden. Apparently, God walked with Adam and Eve daily in the garden, but on this particular day Adam and Eve didn't show up. They were distracted and walked away from God and His will. So, instead of walking with God, they were hiding from God. It's at this point that

God asks a most relevant question, even for us today, "Where are you?" Now He knew where they were, but He wanted them to understand that they were not where they were intended to be—walking with Him.

So, this is MOVEMENT #1—GOD FIRST WANTED TO WALK WITH MAN, BUT MAN WAS BUSY DOING SOMETHING ELSE. God has put a lot of effort in getting you to walk with Him. So, WHERE ARE YOU? Are you doing your part to walk with Him daily or are you distracted, walking away or hiding?

MOVEMENT #2—GOD WANTS TO DWELL AMONG HIS PEO-PLE. God wants to dwell among His people on planet earth. In a very real sense, this is what will distinguish God and His people from all others. In Exodus 25:8 God says, "Then have them make a sanctuary for me and I will dwell among them."

God commands Moses to oversee the building of a sanctuary in which He will dwell. Israel is promised God's very presence. At the very establishment of the nation of Israel, God's presence becomes a fundamental characteristic of the nation's identity. They will be marked by God's presence. To be God's people was to have God's presence. In Exodus 33, following the incident with the golden calf, God promises to have His presence go with Moses and with the people. Moses says, **"Is it not in your going with us, so that we are distinct, I and your people, from every other people on the face of the earth?"** Never before has God dwelt with man in this way.

Man had free fellowship with God in the Garden, but God did not dwell there. God met with Moses on Mt. Sinai in a powerful way, but God did not dwell there. Now God commands Moses to make a tent, a tabernacle, so He could live with them. God wanted to take up residence right in their midst!

Again, this is why God asked Adam and Eve, "Where are you?" And, as His people continued to grow and gather together outside the Garden God was always doing anything He could do to bring His people closer to Himself. But even more than this, He wanted to dwell among His people right here on earth.

And when God shows up among His people, some amazing things happen and people are touched with His loving and healing touch.

This theme of purpose is extended to the very end of the Bible. In the last book of the Bible in Revelation 21:3, it says, **"And I heard a loud voice from the throne saying, 'Look! God's dwelling place is now among the people, and he will dwell with them. They will be his people and God himself will be with them and be their God.'"** This isn't to happen in heaven, but right here on earth.

NOTE God's intention and longing is to come down here, not take a group to go up to heaven. Jesus doesn't teach that He came down to earth to take us up to heaven. God desperately wants to make His presence known right on earth among His people. Rob Bell says that God is saying, "I want to get down there!"

Let me ask you something. Have you ever felt the presence of God as you gather with His people? God is willing to do anything He has to do to get close to you and He wants to do this on planet earth. He is not interested in taking you up to heaven, but to dwell with you right here.

DISCUSSION...

• **Why has this myth become so prevalent in religious circles?**

• **Where did this myth come from?**

• **What direction is God moving — to earth or to heaven? Why?**

The myth that Jesus is all about coming to earth to take people out of here is deeply embedded in the Christian psyche. However, when you examine biblical history and the teachings of Jesus that just isn't the primary direction God is most interested in. He is more interested in the heaven-to-earth connection; He wants it all to happen down here where He dwells among those who love Him.

There are five movements throughout biblical history that illustrate the heaven-to-earth direction of God trying to come down here to be with us. Yesterday I presented the first two. MOVEMENT #1 happened in the Garden where GOD FIRST WANTED TO WALK WITH MAN, BUT MAN WAS BUSY DOING SOMETHING ELSE. After man was kicked out of the Garden, God made His second move toward dwelling among His people here on earth. God commanded Moses to build a tabernacle where He might dwell among His people. Later that portable tabernacle became the Temple in Jerusalem where God dwelt in the Holy of Holies.

There was a third movement where God demonstrated His physical, visible presence to relate to mankind on earth. It's an interesting phenomenon throughout the Bible. It's what many call the "shekinah" glory—the visible presence of God on the earth. This visible manifestation of God is the very presence of God. It's the majestic presence of God in which He dwells with His people. The forms of this visible dwelling place—the shekinah—are many. It could be a brightness, brilliance or splendor. In the Old Testament the Shekinah took the form of light, fire, a cloud, a thick darkness or combination of these in some way. In the New Testament there are new forms altogether!

Let's look at a few of these occurrences.
1. Burning Bush—A bush in the desert caught on fire and yet it did not burn up, because God actually dwelt in this burning bush in front of Moses.

2. The Exodus—The children of Israel were led by day by a cloud and led at night by a pillar of fire—both forms of the visible presence of God.
3. Mount Sinai—While Moses was upon on Sinai, the presence of God was demonstrated by thunders, lightnings, a thick cloud and fire.

4. Tabernacle—We saw this yesterday when God orders them to build an altar or tabernacle where God will dwell in the light and the smoke.

5. Then we come to the most demonstrable form of God's visible presence of all—Jesus—the Son of God. This is best explained in the first

few verses of the Gospel of John: **"In the beginning was the Word, and the Word was with God, and the Word was God. He was with God in the beginning. Through him all things were made; without him nothing was made that has been made. In him was life, and that life was the light of all people. The light shines in the darkness, and the darkness has not overcome it. He was in the world, and though the world was made through him, the world did not recognize him. He came to that which was his own, but his own did not receive him. Yet to all who did receive him, to those who believed in his name, he gave the right to become children of God-children born not of natural descent, nor of human decision or a husband's will, but born of God. The Word became flesh and made his dwelling among us. We have seen his glory, the glory of the one and only [Son], who came from the Father, full of grace and truth.** His name? Jesus!

God will do most anything to get our attention so that you and I will want Him to dwell among us. Well, here He did it. He sent Jesus Who was God in bodily form. All the fullness of God dwells in Jesus. This is why we make so much of watching what Jesus says and does and say and do the same. The ultimate visible, presence of God is in Jesus! All the fullness of God dwells in Him!

The fourth movement of God was when He sent His Spirit to indwell believers as an altar, a tabernacle or Holy of Holies. Jesus departed and the disciples were to be given the Spirit to dwell in them forever! And, ever since Jesus introduced the Spirit to His disciples, we now have the Spirit of God—the presence of God—living in each of us permanently. This is why Paul says in one of the letters written to the Corinthians: "Do you not know that your bodies are temples of the Holy Spirit, who is in you, whom you have received from God? Therefore honor God with your bodies."

There is not a building today where God dwells—a sanctuary, even though many refer to the church auditorium as a sanctuary. You who are followers of Jesus are now the sanctuary—the dwelling place—of God here on earth.

Now, do you remember the reason why God wanted to dwell in an altar, tabernacle or Temple? It was so that God could dwell among His people. I hope you get this. All you have to do is to meditate on this for about 30 seconds and this truth could change your life and your lifestyle forever! You are now the very dwelling place of God on earth.

Don't you get it? The same God of gods Who walked with Adam and Eve in the Garden, Who was in the burning bush, Who was in the cloud by day and the fire by night, Who was revealed in His fullness in bodily form in Jesus of Nazareth. This same God dwells in you who are followers of Jesus. Do you get it? So that He might bring His presence to earth and dwell among us.

The fifth movement of God to go in the direction from heaven to earth is that He wants to walk with you—to show up among us when two or three gather in the name of Jesus. It's all about being the church! God indwells you—His presence on earth is in you who are followers of Jesus. And, when you come together with other followers of Jesus, you are assembling (or churching) in His name. So every time you gather together in His name you are practicing being the church or dwelling place of Jesus.

There is an ultimate movement of God in the future that many times is confused for heaven. It's when the New Jerusalem descends from heaven to earth. You see, from the beginning of time God has desperately desired to dwell among His people and will someday do that right here once the new heavens and the new earth have been created.
I know what you're thinking. There is a passage that seems to say something different. It is from the words of Jesus in John 14 when He says: **"In my Father's house are many rooms; if it were not so, I would have told you. I am going there to prepare a place for you."**

Jesus is going to prepare dwelling places in His Father's house for His disciples. It doesn't mention heaven; that's our assumption. Note then He says, **"And if I go and prepare a place for you, I will come back and take you to be with me that you also may be where I am."** Whatever this dwelling place is, it will be a place where we will be in the presence of Jesus.

Then Jesus says, **"You know the way to the place where I am going."** Thomas quickly says, **"Lord, we don't know where you are going, so how can we know the way?"**

The disciples had missed the point just as we continually do today. There is not a place where Jesus is taking us out of here, therefore no directions are needed. The place or the way Jesus is talking about is summed up in His answer to Thomas: **Jesus answered, "I am the way and the truth and the life. No one comes to the Father except through me."** It's not a dwelling place somewhere out there that we ought to be excited about; it's a person—Jesus! He is the way, the truth and the life. And, through the Spirit dwelling in us, we are in the presence of King Jesus in the Kingdom right here on earth. The place doesn't matter; the Person does! Where two or three are gathered together, Jesus will show up and dwell among us.

Hey, as much as I'd like to get out of here some days, what Jesus has in mind is for me to follow Him wherever He goes and be with Him forever. Now, that's what heaven is all about and Jesus seems to be doing His best to come back here. Right here. Why then would I want to be anywhere else?

DISCUSSION...

Why has this myth become so prevalent in religious circles?

Where did this myth come from?

What direction is God moving—to earth or to heaven? Why?

MYTH #8
JESUS TEACHES WHAT THE WORLD NEEDS NOW IS LOVE

Not only is this myth a popular song; it's a constant and overused anthem of many sermons, articles and conferences. This is so popular that most would attribute it to one of the teachings of Jesus, but it's not. Jesus had something more in mind when it comes to love.

The damage is minimal, yet to embrace this myth is to miss out on the dynamic of what Jesus meant by love. The bottom-line problem is that, love in order to be genuine and powerful must be active.
This one is easy to debunk. FIRST—Love in the teachings of Jesus was a verb—to love. Love as a noun can be discussed; love as a verb must be demonstrated. Love as a noun can generate lots of opinions; love as a verb must be operational—not just talked about, but acted out.

SECOND—Love in the teachings of Jesus was ultimately demonstrated in His act of sacrificial love when He gave Himself up to die on the cross. Jesus came as King of kings to present the new, revolutionary Kingdom. It wasn't a Kingdom of just powerful ideas nor a Kingdom showing off great power; it was a Kingdom of sacrificial love. And, if you are to take up His cross, you must learn to make your life a life of sacrificial love as well.

THIRD—Love in the teachings of Jesus is bi-directional—to love God and to love your neighbor as yourself—and can be practiced by anyone and everyone.

When Jesus was asked to choose the greatest commandment of all, He couldn't just choose one. He offered two, because it's impossible to have one without the other. There are three times this is recorded in the Gospels and each one teaches something a little different.

In Matthew 22:37-40, Jesus replied: **"'Love the Lord your God with** all your heart and with all your soul and with all your mind.' This is the first and greatest commandment. And the second is like it: 'Love your neighbor as yourself.' All the Law and the Prophets hang on these two commandments."** NOTE that upon these two commandments of love all of the Law and the Prophets rest. Loving God and your neighbor are foundational—the most basic actions you can practice.

In Mark 12:28-34, **One of the teachers of the law came and heard them debating. Noticing that Jesus had given them a good answer, he asked him, "Of all the commandments, which is the most important?" "The most important one," answered Jesus, "is this: 'Hear, O Israel: The Lord our God, the Lord is one. Love the Lord your God with all your heart and with all your soul and with all your mind and with all your strength.' The second is this: 'Love your neighbor as yourself.' There is no commandment greater than these."**

"Well said, teacher," the man replied. "You are right in saying that God is one and there is no other but him. To love him with all your heart, with all your understanding and with all your strength, and to love your neighbor as yourself is more important than all burnt offerings and sacrifices." When Jesus saw that he had answered wisely, he said to him, "You are not far from the kingdom of God." NOTE Jesus' comment here: YOU ARE NOT FAR FROM THE KINGDOM OF GOD, when you practice these two commandments.

Then in Luke 10:25-28, **On one occasion an expert in the law stood up to test Jesus. "Teacher," he asked, "what must I do to inherit eternal life?" "What is written in the Law?" he replied. "How do you read it?" He answered, " 'Love the Lord your God with all your heart and with all your soul and with all your strength and with all your mind'; and, 'Love your neighbor as yourself.'" "You have answered correctly," Jesus replied. "Do this and you will live."** NOTE: DO THIS—THESE 2 COMMANDMENTS—AND YOU WILL LIVE!

Do you want to know what you can do to practice the foundational teachings of Jesus, to come close to the Kingdom of God and to really live? It's just so simple: Love God and love your neighbor as yourself.

(Now note this: If you don't love yourself, then your neighbor is in a heap of trouble!)

Jesus didn't teach that what the world needs is more love. That's a myth! No, the world doesn't need more love; it needs more lovers!

DISCUSSION...

What's the difference between the subject of love and being a lover?

Why is it when Jesus was asked to choose the most important commandment, He offered two instead of one?

How do they fit together?

MYTH #9
JESUS PREFERS MEGA-CHURCHES AND MEGA-MINISTRIES

We live in an age of mega-sizing! Bigger is better! Whatever is mega ought to be better than what is small—especially is this true with respect to ministries. The killer question that is always asked of a church or a ministry is: "How many?" The living myth is that Jesus is pleased with these numbers and the masses, too.

One of the great leaders within the mega-church movement, Bill Hybels, has acknowledged that he has been asking the wrong questions. One of those wrong questions is the "How many?" question. It just hasn't produced the transformational change within the church fellowship and has robbed us from asking the right questions. Now, after having participated as pastor of one of the early mega-churches in the US, as a staff member of one of the largest para-church ministries and as a speaker on the largest corporate seminar platform, I have come to understand the great limitations of working with the masses.

The damage of buying into this myth of mega-sizing is threefold:
FIRST—The mega-sizing of the Church hasn't brought about cultural transformation within the US. Rick Warren posed a question that ought to haunt anyone who is concerned about advancing the Jesus movement: "Tim, why is it that, even though we have trained thousands of pastors and now have more mega churches in our country than ever before, we are not making any significant penetration into our culture?" We basically remain at the same numbers within the Church in the US, year after year.

SECOND—The mega-sizing myth of the Western Christian culture serves as a bad example to the followers of Jesus around the world. If we are essentially failing in our country, why export this thinking to the many cultures of the world?

THIRD—The mega-sizing myth has produced thousands upon thousands of spectators who believe they are doing the will of God on planet earth. Spectators—not participators! Ministries then become like the football game—50,000 spectators in the stands, badly in need of exercise and 22 people on the field, badly in need of rest. When you serve as a spectator, it's too easy to substitute attendance for participation—watching and not doing—hearers of the word who delude themselves rather than doers of the word.

I want to make three observations in order to debunk this myth that Jesus prefers the mega-church and mega ministries. FIRST—Jesus spent most of His time and energy with the few and avoiding as much as possible the masses. Now, to be clear, Jesus spoke and fed the masses, but His more common practice was not in that kind of venue. One of my mentors really worked me over on this. I was continually referring to the masses, but he kept correcting me to focus on the individuals. He said, "You don't change the masses; you change individuals one at a time."

SECOND—Jesus spent most of His time with the poor and disenfranchised rather than the powerful. There were powerful people who came to Jesus and were changed, however Jesus tended to seek out the leper, the lame and the blind. When you're into the mega-sizing of your ministry, there will be a tendency to show off the celebrity—the actor, the athlete, the rich and successful as examples. There is nothing wrong with the powerful and influential, but the crowds may not flock in the direction of the poor and disenfranchised. Jesus went there!

THIRD—Jesus was into the power of the few! Instead of going on CNN and seeking to produce mass seminars, mailers and email blasts, Jesus sought out three religious rejects to come and be with Him. And, from this relationship with the three, then the twelve and the seventy-two, the Jesus movement rippled throughout the world and the revolution is still on today!

We are seeing this play out in our ministry. We are focusing on the few and as those few really get it, the message of Jesus spreads like a wildfire. You see, within the context of the few, you are able to really get to know one another and put the principles and teachings into practice. This kind of experience is the taste of reality everyone is longing for. This is the Jesus movement at its best!

Jesus taught: **"Where two or three are gathered together in His name, He will show up."** This is what we want. This is what we desperately need. We need Jesus to show up among us and lead out with His orders and opportunities. You see, Jesus won't be found within the mega-church or mega-ministry as easily as within the context of the few. There's nothing wrong with the mega-church or mega-ministry, but there is something far better that Jesus had in mind.

Jesus prefers showing up when a few are gathered together in His name. If you knew Jesus was going to show up some place this week, wouldn't you want to be there, too?

DISCUSSION...

Are you under the impression that the Jesus movement in the USA is growing and vibrant? What makes you think it is growing?

What are the advantages of the mega-church or mega-ministry today? Disadvantages?

Where is Jesus most comfortable and more apt to show up— large and massive or small and relational?

MYTH #10
JESUS IS HATED BY THE WORLD
AND SO SHOULD HIS DISCIPLES

This is a very common myth within the teachings of Jesus. I lived under its influence and intimidation for years. Jesus was hated by the world and so should His disciples.

The damage here is threefold. FIRST—Those who follow Jesus and His teachings tend to feel intimidated by those who do not. When you feel intimidated by what the world might think of you, then you don't act freely and normally in front of those of the world. If this is true for you, then you will either avoid or withdraw from the people of the world or you might overcompensate and try to control the people of this world and put them into your religious box. So the result is either a holy huddle (we four and no more) or a Christian a power block to force people to obey your rules and standards.

SECOND—The gap between those who follow Jesus becomes so wide that you can tend to think that you have nothing in common. You, who are believers, ride on the white horses while those who are unbelievers ride the dark horses—and they are lame.

THIRD—There is a tendency to "take a stand" for righteousness and to establish sacred noble causes that are all opposed to the world. Several years ago, Bob Briner in his book, *Roaring Lambs*, used to have as a subtitle: "7 Noble Causes That Keep Christians from Changing the World". He listed the following:

1. Squabbling over prayer in public schools!
2. Making Jesus a right-winger!
3. Thwarting the homosexual agenda!
4. Fighting other Christians over doctrinal purity!
5. Shutting down the abortion clinics!
6. Cleaning up television!
7. Fighting for family values!

These may be noble causes, but when they become the focus and the "stand" you must take against the world, they push the world away from Jesus. I've added several more of these noble causes today. By "taking a stand" we set ourselves up as the righteous ones and all others who don't agree are the unrighteous. "Taking a stand" becomes so ugly. It's no wonder Christians are known for their condemning and judgmental spirit and not for the love of Jesus. For example, it's impossible to say to a homosexual, "I love you." Then, to tell him he is going to hell for being a homosexual. You just can't it both ways.

It is a very simple thing to debunk this myth by what Jesus taught His disciples about the world, yet I have stumbled over this passage for years. In John 15 Jesus says, **"If the world hates you, keep in mind that it hated me first."** He goes on to say, **"If they persecuted me, they will persecute you also."** I skipped over this for years, because I found this not to be true in my experience. The world seemed to love me. It was the religious who seemed to always give me the most grief. So, underneath I had this secret fear that I wasn't in sync with Jesus.

Now, it's been my experience that when you are troubled by something in the scriptures, keep reading. In John 16, Jesus clarifies who this world is: **"All this I have told you so that you will not fall away. They will put you out of the synagogue; in fact, the hour is coming when those who kill you will think they are offering a service to God."**

Who is the world? Who are these people? They will put you out of their synagogues—their religious establishments—and will think that they are doing a righteous act—the right thing—as they come against you. They will think they are offering a service to God by their actions. Who are these people? They are the religious ones who are at the helm of their man-made systems and simply Jesus—Jesus plus nothing—interrupts what they already have going for them.

The world is not the secular world system, but the religious. We have more in common with the fellow travelers of the world than with the religious. It's the religious who believe they have it altogether and don't have need for Jesus that Jesus criticized and attacked. He called them vipers and painted tombstones. He really wasn't nice to them, because they are the greatest threat to the Jesus movement today. The non-religious are much more attracted to Jesus and to you as you practice the principles and teachings of Jesus and lovingly touch them.

Well, I'm going to continue hanging out with Jesus and will continue to have my greatest difficulties with the religious, modern-day Pharisees. Even with this spirit of hate, walking with Jesus is the safest place to be. How about you?

DISCUSSION...

Have you ever viewed yourself as being against the world and the world against you?

How have you defined the world?

Does it make sense to you how Jesus describes the world?

MYTH #11
YOU CAN FIND ETERNAL LIFE IN THE SCRIPTURES

From the very beginning there was a human tendency to organize, identify and label the early movement of Jesus' followers. These followers were called the "people of the Way" and "Christians". Later on, the followers of Jesus were organized around the early leadership—elders, bishops and priests. The bishops and the priests were the educated ones and when the Church was organized under Constantine, the priestly hierarchy prevailed.

These hierarchies of priests were naturally placed in positions of authority, because they were the only ones who knew and who could discuss the scriptures. The hierarchy was so highly developed that the position of the Pope emerged as the highest of all authorities. When the Reformation occurred, Luther challenged this system of authority by raising up the scriptures as the ultimate authority, even higher than the religious hierarchy.

But, in my opinion, the Reformation didn't go far enough. The Reformation movement was monumental, but didn't go far enough. The Pope was replaced by the Scriptures and put into the hands of many little popes in authority. In other words, the hierarchy remained in place, though altered a bit and the Scriptures became the ultimate authority.

At that point we re-entered the same perspective and stance of the Pharisees of Jesus' time. They were deeply into the study and memorization of Scripture. Even today, the modern-day Pharisees spend their lives studying the Scriptures.

Within Christianity the Scriptures were first authoritative, then infallible and then they were viewed as inerrant. Each time the Scriptures were being lifted up to a higher and still higher level of authority. The myth here is that the authority and power of the Scriptures can somehow bring a person into eternal life. I believe the biblical Scriptures are highly important and God-breathed, therefore I diligently study them. But there is a great difference in how I see the Scriptures, since Jesus apprehended my life several years ago in a fresh way. The Scriptures are no longer my measuring stick, but Jesus is. Now, I know this is very difficult for many to handle, because we want to have everything written down in order to have something tangible to rely upon. But maybe you have gone a little too far in lifting up the Scriptures to a higher level than Jesus ever intended. Hear me out.

The damage that emerges out of this myth is fourfold: FIRST—The Scriptures are so highly lifted up that there is a tendency to worship the written Word of God. This is called Bibliolatry. I just heard of a pastor who made the inerrant word of God (in the way he interpreted it) the primary rule of his church and that "doctrine will lead our church experience" he says. That's just wrong! The written word is not the head of the body of the church of Jesus—Jesus is.

SECOND—When you lift up the Scriptures too high, you tend to believe that the right understanding of Scriptures is most important for a person's eternal future. Without the right understanding of the Scriptures you may be left behind at the end of time. This has proven to be the most divisive methodology ever—I'm right and you're wrong. And, this divisiveness is most ugly and does not traffic in the love of Jesus.

THIRD—When you lift up the Scriptures too high, you tend to think that our youth today who are leaving Christianity can be won back by teaching them the Scriptures in a more effective way. It's teaching, teaching, teaching more of the right doctrine.

FOURTH—When you lift up the Scriptures too high, you tend to miss the only way to possess eternal life—the person of Jesus. The tendency is to equate the Gospel with a set of beliefs or a system of doctrines and to miss out on the dynamic of a personal, faith, followship kind of relationship with Jesus.

To debunk this myth, I want to use the exact words of Jesus as He addressed the Pharisees on this subject. In John 5:39, **Jesus says, "You**

diligently study the Scriptures because you think that by them you possess eternal life. These are the Scriptures that testify about me, yet you refuse to come to me to have life." This is why Paul explains how faith comes to us. He says, **"Faith comes by hearing and hearing by the spoken word of Christ."** Faith comes not by studying and memorizing bible texts, but only to those who seek after Jesus and listen to what He says.

The Scriptures cannot give you eternal life—not at all! The study of the Scriptures is important, but only as they give you Jesus. By the way, the Scriptures Jesus was referring to here are the only Scriptures that they had at that time—the Old Testament. Luke relates the story of Jesus walking with a couple of disciples after the resurrection on the road to Emmaus: And beginning with Moses and all the Prophets, he explained to them what was said in all the Scriptures concerning himself. And later Luke says, **Then he opened their minds so they could understand the Scriptures**.

Remember, in the 1st chapter of the Gospel of John: In the beginning was the word and the word was with God and the word was God. He was in the beginning with God. It doesn't say "IT was in the beginning with God, but HE—JESUS—was in the beginning with God." Then, a few verses later, John says, **"And He (Jesus) became flesh and dwelt among us."**

Searching for eternal life in the Scriptures will prove to be futile. Yet, many find it easier than seeking after Jesus personally. It's so much easier to follow a list of do's and don'ts; it's very difficult to relate to Jesus.

It's all about Jesus—always was, is and always will be. The Good News or the Gospel is Jesus. The Kingdom is Jesus. And, only Jesus can give you eternal life. In fact, Jesus is eternal life. Follow Jesus and you can enjoy that life beginning right now.

DISCUSSION...

Why do people tend to worship the Bible?

Can you see how your view of the Bible can put Jesus aside, so that you are seeking life from the Scriptures than Jesus Himself?

What are some safeguards to keep this from happening?

MYTH #12
JESUS MOSTLY TAUGHT ABOUT THE CHURCH

It just seems to be a logical thing. If you've grown up in Church or out-side of Church, you certainly would not be surprised at or balk at the statement, "Jesus mostly taught about the Church." But that statement is a myth; it is not a true statement. Jesus only mentioned the church three times in two passages.

Matthew 16:18—**And I tell you that you are Peter, and on this rock I will build my *church*, and the gates of Hades will not overcome it.**

Matthew 18:17—**If he refuses to listen to them, tell it to the *church*; and if he refuses to listen even to the *church*, treat him as you would a pagan or a tax collector**.

The damage is threefold: FIRST—By believing this myth you will find yourself with an emphasis Jesus never intended or embraced. The term "church" is not a special, holy word. I was taught in my first Greek class that it was created as a highly charged, powerful term, meaning "called-out ones". It was presented to us as a spiritual term—a Christian term, but in actuality it wasn't. However, it was used for any gathering—a city council or gathering for any specific purpose.

SECOND—By believing this myth you might begin to believe that be-ing a member of a Church and identifying with a Church are at the core of what is at the heart of Jesus.

THIRD—By believing this myth you will miss what Jesus thought was more important—the Kingdom. Why do we preach and teach the "church", when Jesus didn't? The only thing Jesus calls the gospel is the Kingdom—the gospel of the Kingdom. When you are more conversant with the Kingdom, you will come to know that this is not only the good news; it is the BEST NEWS ever!

Why do you think we emphasize the church & minimize the Kingdom? I think there is a sense that one or a few can control the organized Church, but only God is in control of the Kingdom. Also, the Church is visible and easier to relate to; the Kingdom is invisible and therefore difficult to get your arms around. Since the Kingdom is Jesus' major theme throughout His ministry and since we want to walk, think, love and talk like Jesus, then our theme is best viewed as JESUS and the KINGDOM.

The Kingdom is the rule of God on planet earth both personally and in community. The church is a simple gathering together in the name of Jesus. It is simply a gathering of followers of Jesus. This simple gathering of followers of Jesus on any day and at any location is a church. These gatherings revolve around four ingredients—fellowship, food, prayer and the apostles' teachings. The only one of these ingredients that might throw you a bit might be the apostles' teachings. We see this as what had been passed on through the early disciples about Jesus and the Kingdom. So, since the Kingdom is the rule and presence of God on planet earth, you could also think of it as wherever the King is, there is the Kingdom. The King and the Kingdom are inseparable. Therefore a good way to view the Kingdom is Christ-likeness universalized.

The Kingdom is universal and everywhere. The church is a local gathering of followers of Jesus who are seeking, sharing in and spreading the gospel of Jesus and the Kingdom. The church is not everywhere, but localized and limited to those who choose to gather together. The Kingdom is everywhere and unlimited in its impact on society. The Kingdom is not waiting for a local gathering to be established in order to have its effect. The Kingdom is already there in every country and in every culture.

By the way, this triggers a lot of implications on the prevalent thinking of "planting churches". The message of Jesus and the Kingdom is spreading like a mustard seed, starting as small little groups and growing. It's also spreading like leaven in a lump of dough, growing irreversibly in our world. Wherever you see Jesus and the Kingdom breaking out in a culture or neighborhood or group of people, get there as soon as possible and encourage them.

Our theme then is the theme of Jesus—it's the person of Jesus and the Kingdom of God. Note this theme throughout the book of the *Acts of Jesus*.

1. In Acts 1, it says, ***After* his suffering, he presented himself to them and gave many convincing proofs that he was alive. He appeared to them over a period of forty days and spoke about the kingdom of God**. Jesus was concerned to present Himself to His disciples personally and then He spent these last few days teaching them about the Kingdom. He felt it was that important.

2. In Acts 8, Philip was teaching in the area of Samaria and it says, **But when they believed Philip as he proclaimed the good news of the kingdom of God and the name of Jesus the Christ, they were baptized, both men and women**. Note again, the theme is the name of Jesus and the Kingdom of God.

3. In Acts 28, when Paul was under house arrest in rented quarters in Rome, many came to meet with him. Note what he felt was most important: **He witnessed to them from morning till evening, explaining about the kingdom of God and from the Law of Moses and from the Prophets he tried to persuade them about Jesus**. Later in the same chapter it says, **For two whole years Paul stayed there in his own rented house and welcomed all who came to see him. He proclaimed the kingdom of God and taught about the Lord Jesus the Christ—with all boldness and without hindrance!**

Note that none of these men—Jesus, Philip and Paul—felt it was important to teach anyone about the Church. It was all about Jesus and the Kingdom. So, why do we spend most of our time and energy discussing and teaching the many themes of the Church, when Jesus didn't? Why do we do that?

DISCUSSION...

Is the fact that Jesus taught so little about the church a shocker to you?

Can you see how this myth has been applied and therefore responsible for misdirecting so many followers of Jesus?

How would you define the Kingdom?

MYTH #13
JESUS TEACHES HATE FOR FAMILY MEMBERS

One of the most offensive attacks leveled at Christians and Christianity is this myth—"JESUS TEACHES HATE." Even Christian clergy and other Christians yield to this attack. When I was speaking at a major event for the Dalai Lama, there were several hundred clerics in attendance. When one of the American Buddhist committee members called me to ask if I would be willing to speak at this event, I quickly accepted. But before I did, this event organizer said they were looking for someone to represent Christianity and thought I would do a good job. I explained to him that I don't represent Christianity very well. He then said, "Well, what would you represent?" I said, "I am just a stubborn follower of Jesus."

Of the fourteen speakers on the platform, most were Buddhist, Muslim, a Hindu nun, a Jewish rabbi, a famous religion historian, two Christian clerics (an Episcopalian and a Catholic priest) and a follower of Jesus. What was so disappointing to me were the remarks made by the two Christian clerics. One disappointment was that neither of them even mentioned the name of Jesus—not once. The other was that one of them apologized in his speech to the other clerics for the teaching of hate in the New Testament and quoted what Jesus said in Luke 14: **"If anyone comes to me and does not hate father and mother, wife and children, brothers and sisters—yes, even life itself—such a person cannot be my disciple."**

If Jesus is identified with this statement calling for hate in the sense we know hate, then the damage is great as people hear this and are considering this Jesus. Hate taught by Jesus makes Him no better than the ugly hate and condemnation of the many religious factions in our world. Christians certainly own that judgmental attitude in the USA.

For years I have taught this as a Hebrew idiom that is an expression of comparison. I have always said it means: "By comparison, your relationship with Jesus is so outstanding that all other relationships look like hate." That seemed to work for those who were listening, however something just didn't set well in my gut. I still didn't like the One Who is known for the greatest expressions of love ever being associated with that term, "hate".

Recently, I've been introduced to a concept I've completely overlooked. My friend, Congressman Mark Siljander, a student of many languages, has shown me through his studies in Aramaic what Jesus most likely said. You know, Jesus spoke in Aramaic and there is a written Aramaic version of the Gospels. In the Aramaic "hate" is not the word. What Jesus actually said was: "If anyone comes to me and does not set aside all other relationships, such a person cannot be my disciple." In other words, it's not "hate", but "set aside" that Jesus says. This is so much more pleasing and consistent with the loving Jesus I know. It makes more sense, yet still a very strong requirement for counting yourself as a disciple of Jesus. (By the way, Mark's book, *A Deadly Misunderstanding*, is being released on October 7th and I heartily recommend it.)

Let's go through all three requirements Jesus offers to be a disciple. Luke 14 has the entire context. FIRST—This is the priority requirement. You must set aside all other relationships and make them subordinate to your relationship with Jesus. He must be the preeminent one—the priority of your life. Large crowds were traveling with Jesus, and turning to them he said: **"If anyone comes to me and does not set aside father and mother, wife and children, brothers and sisters—yes, even life itself—such a person cannot be my disciple."**

Note that there were lots of people following Jesus at this time—crowds! He wanted each of them to not just go along with the crowds, but to make Him the definite priority of their lives. He didn't say that if you don't do this, you cannot be my good disciple, but you cannot be my disciple at all.

SECOND—This is the perseverance requirement. You will follow after Jesus as your priority NO MATTER WHAT. Jesus says, **"And whoever does not carry their cross and follow me cannot be my disciple."** No matter what happens, Jesus is number one for you. He uses the image of carrying your cross. The cross of Jesus was the greatest expression of sacrificial love ever. To be a disciple of Jesus you must carry your cross of sacrificial love with you wherever you go—persistently. That is one our primary reasons for being.

THIRD—This is the possessions requirement. Jesus says, **"In the same way, those of you who do not give up everything you have cannot be my disciples."** Jesus is not saying that you are to give over all your possessions, but to give them up. I see this as renouncing the ownership of all you have. You really don't own what you have. You are a manager or steward of what God has allowed you to collect. Jesus wants you to realize this and be willing to give up all you have for Jesus and the Kingdom.

It's even more than this. You are not just to give up everything you have, but all you are as well—your very existence. He owns it all—you and all of your stuff! It's learning to wear the cloak of materialism loosely and to live your life as one who is owned and directed by Jesus.

So, Jesus isn't into hate. He doesn't require you or want you to hate at all. That's a nasty and unfortunate myth. But Jesus does present some very tough requirements to be a disciple who is a follower of Him.
Jesus ends these requirements with a familiar saying of His. He says, **"Whoever has ears to hear, let them hear."** You might even say that the very first requirement Jesus is looking for before anything else is: ARE YOU INTERESTED—interested enough to listen—to have ears to hear and eyes to see? Are you interested?

DISCUSSION...

Have you ever felt uneasy about Jesus saying He requires His disciples to hate family members?

Can you see what His intent was in this requirement?

How do you respond to the three requirements Jesus teaches for you to be a disciple?

MYTH #14
GOD DWELLS IN HOLY BUILDINGS TODAY

I have mentioned this myth before from a different angle. This myth is repeatedly taught in two ways. The first comes through the constant referrals about the auditorium within a church building, calling that large assembly room the sanctuary. The second way it is taught is the signage at most church campuses. You will find the term "sanctuary", pointing out where the church will assemble.

Essentially this myth is saying that when you go to your religious house of worship, God actually dwells there. The building is His sanctuary or dwelling place. In many Christian "sanctuaries" the actual place of dwelling is thought to be up at the altar. Therefore, congregants are encouraged to go forward to take communion, to meet the Lord in prayer, to receive salvation, to be healed or rededicate your life.

So, people today are expected to believe that God dwells in holy buildings—Churches, Mosques, Temples and Synagogues. But Jesus and a special teaching from Paul in Athens debunk this myth soundly.

FIRST—Jesus' conversation with the woman at the well debunks this myth (John 4): **"Woman,"** Jesus replied, **"believe me,** *a time is coming when you will worship the Father neither on this mountain nor in Jerusalem.* **You Samaritans worship what you do not know; we worship what we do know, for salvation is from the Jews.** *Yet a time is coming and has now come when the true worshipers will worship the Father in the Spirit and in truth, for they are the kind of worshipers the Father seeks. God is spirit, and his worshipers must worship in the Spirit and in truth."*

The woman said, "I know that Messiah" (called Christ) **"is coming. When he comes, he will explain everything to us." Then Jesus declared, "I, the one speaking to you—I am he."** Jesus, the Christ—the Messiah, has shown up and if you will watch and listen, you will come to understand that Jesus has explained everything to us. Here with the woman at the well, Jesus has made it clear that certain holy locations like mountains or buildings will not be sufficient to be the dwelling place of God, because God dwells in the invisibility of spirit and truth.

SECOND—In Athens Paul speaks to a non-Jewish audience and explains the nature of God and where He doesn't dwell. This is recorded by Luke in Acts 17: **While Paul was waiting for them in Athens, he was greatly distressed to see that the city was full of idols. So he reasoned in the synagogue with both Jews and God-fearing Greeks, as well as in the marketplace day by day with those who happened to be there. A group of Epicurean and Stoic philosophers began to debate with him. Some of them asked, "What is this babbler trying to say?" Others remarked, "He seems to be advocating foreign gods." They said this because Paul was preaching the good news about Jesus and the resurrection. Then they took him and brought him to a meeting of the Areopagus, where they said to him, "May we know what this new teaching is that you are presenting? You are bringing some strange ideas to our ears, and we would like to know what they mean." (All the Athenians and the foreigners who lived there spent their time doing nothing but talking about and listening to the latest ideas.)**

Paul then stood up in the meeting of the Areopagus and said: "People of Athens! I see that in every way you are very religious. For as I walked around and looked carefully at your objects of worship, I even found an altar with this inscription: TO AN UNKNOWN GOD. So you are ignorant of the very thing you worship—and this is what I am going to proclaim to you.

"The God who made the world and everything in it is the Lord of heaven and earth and does not live in temples built by hands. And he is not served by human hands, as if he needed anything. Rather, he himself gives everyone life and breath and everything else. From one man he made all the nations, that they should inhabit the whole earth; and he marked out their appointed times in history and the boundaries of their lands. God did this so that they would seek him

and perhaps reach out for him and find him, though he is not far from any one of us. 'For in him we live and move and have our being.' As some of your own poets have said, 'We are his offspring.'

"Therefore since we are God's offspring, we should not think that the divine being is like gold or silver or stone—an image made by human design and skill. In the past God overlooked such ignorance, but now he commands all people everywhere to repent. For he has set a day when he will judge the world with justice by the man he has appointed. He has given proof of this to everyone by raising him from the dead." The God of heaven and earth cannot be limited to dwell in buildings or idols.

THIRD—Jesus' teachings debunk this myth, when He teaches about sending His Spirit to His disciples (John 14): **"If you love me, keep my commands. And I will ask the Father, and he will give you another advocate to help you and be with you forever—the Spirit of truth. The world cannot accept him, because it neither sees him nor knows him. But you know him, for he lives with you and will be in you."**

Jesus replied, "Anyone who loves me will obey my teaching. My Father will love them, and we will come to them and make our home (our dwelling place) with them."

So, when you go into a holy building, that is not the dwelling place of God on earth today as it once was with the great Temple in Jerusalem. God, through the Spirit of Jesus, now dwells in you. You are the sanctuary of God—His dwelling place on earth. The challenge? To walk like it, talk like it and act like it.

DISCUSSION...

Have you grown up with the term "sanctuary" used to describe the auditorium where you meet for your religious services?

Have you ever felt like there was something especially "holy" about the upfront location of your auditorium—the altar?

How does this kind of thinking limit your relationship with God?

What implications become evident if you are the holy dwelling of God?

MYTH #15
"GOING TO CHURCH" IS JESUS' IDEA

This myth flows out of the last one — GOD DWELLS IN HOLY BUILD-INGS TODAY. The myth here lies in the terminology of "going to church". This was never the intent of the Jesus movement. If God truly is dwelling in a building where the organized Church gathers, then we must get over there right away.

The myth emerges out of a frequently quoted passage in Hebrews (10:25): **and let us consider how to stimulate one another to love and good deeds, not forsaking our own assembling together, as is the habit of some, but encouraging one another; and all the more as you see the day drawing near**. This has become the Christian mantra for making sure everyone goes to Church whenever the doors are open. Years ago there was a man on my staff who wanted to have each of our fellowship fill out a card to register their attendance and then call those who didn't show up to sort of discipline them toward getting their act together to not miss church any more. There is definitely something to staying in communication with those in your fellowship in a personal sort of way, but not to badger them to get into line to go to church.

The damage of this myth is threefold: FIRST — The idea of going to church limits God and His presence to a location.

SECOND — The idea of going to church misses the concept and practice of the presence of the Kingdom.

THIRD — The idea of going to church leads to building monuments rather than joining a movement.

I want to debunk this myth in the following ways: FIRST — The myth distracts you away from the most miraculous thing that has ever happened to mankind — GOD DWELLS IN YOU. So, your walk with Jesus and with others is not that you are to "go to church", but to be the church of Jesus. The Kingdom—the presence of the King—is already among you all, therefore practice it—live it out in your life—live out the King's presence in your life together. You are the church of Jesus as you gather together anywhere in His name.

SECOND—Going to church as a location rather than a movement takes away the active, revolutionary nature of what Jesus intended for those who gather in His name. In Matthew 16 Jesus makes an incredible declaration. He says, **"I will build my church and the gates of Hades will not overcome it or prevail against it."** This sounds like the gates of Hades will not be able to bring it down. Now, if Jesus is talking about a church location or local organization, then He was mistaken. You see, many churches are brought down, defeated and closed down every week in the USA. *The Message* by Eugene Peterson nails the meaning of this passage and captures the essence of the original word "overcome" when it says, **"This is the rock on which I will put together my church, a church so expansive with energy that not even the gates of hell will be able to keep it out."**

Do the see the difference? It is not that the gates of Hades will be powerful enough to overcome the church, but that the gates of Hades will not be able to withstand or keep it out or stop the powerful thrust and energy of the Jesus movement. The powerful thrust of the church of Jesus gathering together as a movement is due to spiritual transformation through the power of Jesus in each follower's life. This is why the church cannot be viewed as a distribution center for religious aspirin and other consumer goods. The church of Jesus cannot become a place where people only go to baptisms, marriages and funerals—only to be hatched, matched and dispatched.

We live in the age of the hungry spirit. We may not be a human being having a spiritual experience, but a spiritual being having a human experience. People are searching for authenticity. Jesus is the authentic way, truth and the life. Following Jesus is not a belief system; it's all about a Person and how to follow Him. What is needed is a spiritual revolution—a revolution that gets us back to the simplicity and purity of devotion to Jesus. The simple gathering of followers of Jesus on any day and at any location is a church. These gatherings revolve around four ingredients—fellowship, food, prayer and the apostles' teachings or the discussions around the teachings of Jesus and the Kingdom.

So if we who are followers of Jesus are the church of Jesus—the gathering of Jesus, and it isn't about "going to church" but "being the church", what does Jesus want us to do with the organized Church today? Reading through the 5 gospels (Matthew-Mark-Luke-John-Acts) it is clear what Jesus and the disciples did with the "organized Church". Let's view the synagogue as the organized Church. There are three observations that seem most relevant to us:

1. You don't find Jesus or the disciples bashing the Synagogue (Church).
2. You don't find Jesus or the disciples starting new Synagogues (Churches), because of inadequate teaching or worship.
3. You find Jesus and the disciples using the Synagogues (Churches) to worship together, to enjoy the reading of the word and then orbiting around them.

Several years ago I read a book, *ORBITING THE GIANT HAIRBALL...A Corporate Fool's Guide To Surviving With Grace* by Gordon MacKenzie. MacKenzie worked at Hallmark Greeting Cards for 30 years in the creative department. He found that he was unable to be very creative, if he had to spend his time in corporate meetings. So he learned to orbit around the corporate bureaucracy and not be entangled in it, freeing him to create. He also makes it clear that the hairball was absolutely necessary. Without it there was nothing to power the orbit and the hairball paid the bills.

Remember the insight from the book **Orbiting The Giant Hairball**? This is exactly what the early fellowships of Jesus did. They participated in the Synagogue, yet they were in orbit around their Synagogue, their communities and around the marketplace. They went to Synagogue (Church) every Sabbath, yet they were there for a higher purpose—a Kingdom purpose. They were there to introduce more and more people to the preeminence of Jesus. When interest was expressed, they invited them to eat together and practice the presence of the Kingdom.

Many of the mega Churches today realize how important it is to move their members into a smaller gathering, so they put a lot of energy into small groups. Some of these small groups practice the preeminence of Jesus and the presence of the Kingdom and some don't. If the groups gather in the name of Jesus and become more like family, Jesus shows up and great things happen. Small groups that are study groups tend to learn about Jesus and not get to know Him and His Kingdom community sitting around the room.

Here's the bottom-line. Don't spend your time, treasure and energies building the church; that's Jesus job. He said He will build His church. Don't build the church or go to church, revolving your life around a monument. That monument may someday be empty as the cathedrals of Europe. BE THE CHURCH OF JESUS! Now that's a powerful movement that cannot be stopped and will always be filled with the love and power of Jesus and His Kingdom.

DISCUSSION...

What's the difference between going to Church and being the church?

Who is in charge of building the church of Jesus?
Who is in charge of building your local Church?

What does it mean to orbit around the Church (Synagogue)?

MYTH #16
JESUS CAN ONLY BE TRULY REVEALED
THROUGH THE BIBLE

As a kid, a minister told me that only the King James was genuinely effective in sharing the Good News of Jesus. He even shared with us that no matter what passage you share with others, the only passages to actually effect salvation were these. And then, he handed out a card with a series of King James passages and he made it clear that no other passages and no other version would "work". Later a joke we shared with one another while in graduate school was, "If the King James was good enough for Jesus, then it is good enough for me!" Naturally, the joke was that the King James was not even created until nearly 1600 years after Jesus.

This myth is a serious one of control. We just want to think that we own the only way to Jesus and that is our favorite version of the bible. The damage is twofold: FIRST—This myth can lead you into a position that you might shut the door of the Kingdom to those with whom God is working.

SECOND—This myth puts God in a box and will not allow Him to work in any other way than your particular version of the bible or the bible itself.

To debunk this myth I'd like to offer several examples. FIRST—The only bible or scriptures available at the time of Jesus' ministry was the Hebrew Torah, historical books, the wisdom literature and the prophets. So, how was Jesus revealed?

SECOND—Jesus was revealed through the teachings of the Hebrew and Aramaic Scriptures. Remember, Jesus, after His resurrection, revealed Himself by sharing with the two disciples walking to Emmaus. He revealed Himself by explaining the portrait of the Messiah throughout the then known Scriptures.

In the 24th chapter of Luke, after the resurrection, Jesus appeared to the disciples. Let's listen in: He said to them, "This is what I told you while I was still with you: Everything must be fulfilled that is written about me in the Law of Moses, the Prophets and the Psalms." Then he opened their minds so they could understand the Scriptures. I long to revisit the Old Testament Scriptures with this in mind that I might see Jesus more clearly—that my mind by be opened for a fuller understanding.

THIRD—Jesus is revealed by your life of following Him. Jesus says in Matthew 5 that people can see God and respond positively to Him through your good works. He says, "In the same way, let your light shine before others, that they may see your good deeds and glorify your Father in heaven."

Paul writes to the followers of Jesus in Corinth and challenges them with the same kind of thinking on how Jesus is seen: You yourselves are our letter, written on our hearts, known and read by everyone. You show that you are a letter from Christ, the result of our ministry, written not with ink but with the Spirit of the living God, not on tablets of stone but on tablets of human hearts. (II Corinthians 3)

FOURTH—Jesus is revealed by fulfilling the Law and traditions. Jesus makes it clear that He has not come to abolish the Law in any way, but to fulfill it. This literally means to make it full or to fill it up. I envision the Law of Moses as an empty container with a certain structure to it and Jesus fills it full. He is the fulfillment of it! I believe Jesus is the ultimate fulfillment of every religious structure that is filled with the various laws, values and dreams. Jesus can fill up any empty container in the same way.

I heard this from a friend: All roads don't lead to Jesus, but Jesus leads to all roads. And, He fulfills every desire and longing within the hearts of every culture of the world. In Ecclesiastes 3 it says, He has made everything beautiful in its time. He has also set eternity in the human heart; yet no one can fathom what God has done from beginning to end. God has already set the longing for eternity in the heart of man.

FIFTH—Jesus is revealed by the use of pagan and other religious writings as well as supernatural experiences. In Acts 17 Paul quotes a local poet who wrote for the religious ceremonies of worship for Zeus and Mollech, yet Paul uses it to reveal Jesus to the crowd in Athens. We are finding Jesus revealed in the ancient writings of the Muslim Koran, the Hindu Vedas, and within the early writings of Buddhism and the religious thinking of the Polynesian people regarding their Creator-God. People in some of the remote parts of the world are seeing Jesus in dreams and visions. Hey, I don't even pretend to understand it all, but I know people by the millions are coming into a personal relationship with Jesus and following Him.

SIXTH—Jesus is revealed by the spoken word of God. This is not the logos word of God, but the rhema word of God. In Romans 10:17 it says, Faith comes by hearing and hearing by the spoken (rhema) word of God.

Think about it! When the massive movement of Jesus in China multiplied into the millions without bibles, how was Jesus revealed? He was revealed by the spoken word of God about the Good News of Jesus. Even in the early movement of Jesus, He is primarily revealed by word of mouth—by the personal testimonies of those who had already encountered Him.

SEVENTH—Jesus is revealed by the two natural lights—conscience on the inside and creation on the outside. We see this in Romans 1: **For the wrath of God is revealed from heaven against all ungodliness and unrighteousness of men who suppress the truth in unrighteousness, because that which is known about God is evident within them; for God made it evident to them. NOTE people tend to suppress the truth and that truth is known to mankind first by what God made evident within them. This might be called conscience or God-consciousness; these are the moral motions that are already in every person's heart—knowing what is right and wrong. God revealed this to us in our hearts.**

God also made it evident to them to know about Him and His plan for them in the creation: For since the creation of the world His invisible attributes, His eternal power and divine nature, have been clearly seen, being understood through what has been made, so that they are without excuse. For even though they knew God, they did not honor Him as God or give thanks, but they became futile in their speculations, and their foolish heart was darkened.

So, it's a myth that only the bible is the place that Jesus is revealed. The way I see it is that the Creator-God of the universe is relentless and will do whatever He can to reveal Jesus to everyone who has ears to hear and eyes to see. Are you listening and watching?

DISCUSSION...

What does it mean to put God in a box?

What is the most common way you see people putting God in a box?

Of the seven ways God is revealed which ones resonate most with you?

MYTH #17
JESUS WANTS US TO CHANGE THE WORLD

This is a myth that penetrates ministry efforts around the world. There is a constant man-made effort to organize the message of Jesus into a standardized methodology. So, over the years many methods have been created and promoted to be the best ways, and sometimes the only ways, ministry is done. Examples of these methods are gospel tracts, such as the "Four Spiritual Laws", altar calls at the end of the church service, conversion tactics on the mission field or use of a certain bible translation. These methods are employed to do what we think Jesus wants us to do—to change the world.

The damage is fourfold: FIRST—If you think you must change the world, you will create an agenda for every person you approach. If a person is from a different religious persuasion, then your agenda is to talk them out of their religion and into yours. If a person believes in evolution, then your agenda is to argue with him about creation. If a person is doing something you want him to change, then your agenda is to figure out a way to change him. There are so many noble causes in our society that have become major agendas that get in the way of really changing the world—like fighting over the homosexual agenda or fighting abortion or fighting over family value issues or arguing over politics.

SECOND—If you think you must change the world, you believe you are "right" and disrespect all others from different backgrounds.

THIRD—If you think you must change the world, then you may not include the only one who can change those in your world of influence—Jesus.

FOURTH—If you think you must change the world, then you tend to think you are in charge of the results and actually making the changes happen.

To debunk this myth we need only observe the life and methodology of Jesus. Jesus always worked with the needs of the person He encountered. In other words, Jesus allowed the needs of the person to dictate His approach.

Therefore, Jesus never approached two people in the same way. His relationship with each person is so unique.

No matter what the need was that Jesus encountered, He was always the answer. There may be a physical or mental healing, but He, personally, was the solution to everyone's problem. I love the theoretical conversation that goes like this:

Man: I have a problem; it's me!
Jesus: I have the answer; it's Me!

Jesus doesn't want us to change the world. That's a myth. Jesus is the only one who is able to change a person's heart and therefore the only one who can change the world. All we can do is to introduce Jesus into the situation with the world around us. We must become convinced that our primary and only effective role is to advance the conversation of Jesus in our world.

Congressman Mark Siljander has summarized the approach he has used in international negotiations with some of the most difficult situations in our world. It is a strategy for introducing Jesus—the universal change-agent—into most any encounter. (Siljander's new book, ***A Deadly Misunderstanding***, is to be released on October 7th, which contains the essence of this approach.) The four phases of Siljander's approach are the following. First, he says if you want to see real change, it's important to begin with no agenda whatsoever. If you have an agenda, you will trigger a variety of defenses and will face major resistance. Don't approach someone with what's on your mind, but seek what's on his or her mind.

Secondly, he says if you want to see real change, you must incorporate unconditional love. When you show genuine love to someone, you will respect them and their differing positions they hold. You don't have to agree with them; just love them in the spirit and specificity of I Corinthians 13.

Thirdly, he says if you want to see real change, you must introduce Jesus without religious baggage. It's in the spirit of Jesus that you can truly love someone unconditionally. The power of Jesus' name introduces a dynamic into the equation that is immeasurable. At the name of Jesus, something good and supernatural happens.

Fourthly, he says if you want to see real change, you must count on the Spirit of Jesus to make the changes in the person's heart. In other words, you continue to get out of the way, once you've introduced Jesus, and watch Him work. Leave the results to Him.

This strategy works, not only in the toughest of international negotiations, but in your family, in your community and in your business. Jesus doesn't want us to change anyone anywhere. He wants us to touch people He brings to us with no agenda and unconditional love as we introduce Jesus into the mix and count on His Spirit to make the changes. You and I aren't going to change anybody, but Jesus can make that change in everyone you encounter in His time and in His way.

DISCUSSION...

What is wrong with you thinking you must change the world?

Can you define Congressman Siljander's approach to bring about transformation in international negotiations? Which one stands out to you?

MYTH #18
JESUS WANTS YOU TO BE HOOOLY

Now before you get too upset with me and this myth, it's not so much how it is spelled, but how it is said: HOOOLY has a super-spiritual connotation to it. But Jesus doesn't want you to be a super-saint or a super-spiritual person. That's a myth.

The damage is threefold: FIRST—To be HOOOLY sets up a level of spirituality that is unattainable and intimidating.

SECOND—To be HOOOLY sets up a 1st class Christianity versus those who are 2nd class or coach. Talk about shutting the door of the Kingdom on people!

THIRD—To be HOOOLY is to operate under a gross misunderstanding of what "holy" really means. It's usually half-understood. Literally, "holy" means to be separated unto God for His mission. However, where I grew up to be "holy" was shortened to mean "be separated". The way it was applied to me was that we are to be separated—different—from the rest of the world. It was definitely a "We four and no more kind of lifestyle!" We were an established holy huddle in our community. We were different because we didn't do certain things—attend movies, drink any alcohol, dance or even skate to secular music. We were different all right and successfully turned people away from the attractive, irresistible Jesus.

To be HOOOLY is just the opposite of what Jesus intended. He mostly used the term "holy" to describe the Holy Spirit, holy angels, and the Holy Place—the Temple. As I said earlier the term "holy" means to be separated or set apart unto God for His mission. The Spirit is holy. The angels are holy. Even the Temple was holy—separated unto God for His mission.

Jesus was most upset and angry with those who continually acted

HOOOLY and missed out on true holiness. He rebuked those super-spiritual, nit-picker, hair-splitting, feather-plucking, hyper-critical leaders who set themselves up as the religious examples of righteousness. They majored in the minors and minored in the majors. They professed righteousness without possessing it and they did it by carefully following their traditions, man-made commandments and religious causes. This kept them set apart and separated from the rest of the world. As they worked hard to keep the 613 laws—248 commandments and 365 prohibitions—they just kept drawing the condemnation of men on the righteous acts before God.

The Scriptures taught holiness, but the meaning of it was not to just be set apart and be different, gathering yourselves into a holy huddle.

In the Hebrew Scriptures it is clear that God wants those who claim to be related to Him to be holy. In Leviticus 11:44-45 it says: I am the LORD your God; consecrate yourselves and be holy, because I am holy. **I am the LORD who brought you up out of Egypt to be your God; therefore be holy, because I am holy**. Later in Leviticus 20:26 it says: **You are to be holy to me because I, the LORD, am holy, and I have set you apart from the nations to be my own**. Paul and Peter in the New Testament speak of being **"called to be holy"** and **"make every effort to live in peace with all men and be holy"**. Peter says in his first letter: But just as he who called you is holy, so be holy in all you do.

Even though Jesus doesn't command His followers to be holy, in the spirit of what is understood by the references in Leviticus and by the few references to be holy by a few of Jesus' disciples, Jesus does actually teach holiness—to be set apart unto God for His mission. I think Jesus is all about teaching those who want to be His disciples how to be holy. He does this by His two most revolutionary words: FOLLOW ME! In contrast to the super-spiritual community of the Pharisees and the Sadducees, Jesus invited the people who were interested in following Him to: **"Come to Me, all who are weary and heavy-laden, and I will give you rest. Take My yoke upon you and learn from Me, for I am gentle and humble in heart, and YOU WILL FIND REST FOR YOUR SOULS. For My yoke is easy and My burden is light."**

Do you see it? They were into being HOOOLY and were actually a holy huddle who missed out on the second part of the definition of holiness—to be separated unto God for His mission. To be holy is to be set apart for God's use and purposes. Jesus invites us to follow Him—to be aligned with Him in such a way that we are on the mission He has planned for us—to walk, talk, think and love like Jesus.

Jesus puts it in a simple way when He says, **"If you hear my words and practice them, you will be like a wise man who builds his house on a rock and no matter what beats against your house, it will stand firm."**

Jesus doesn't want us to be HOOOLY, but holy—set apart to follow Him.

DISCUSSION...

What is the definition of holy you have embraced over the years?

What problems emerge because of your old definition?

What is the definition of holy?

MYTH #19
'JESUS PLUS NOTHING' IS SIMPLER AND EASIER TO LIVE

My favorite verse that Paul penned is in the second letter he wrote to the followers of Jesus in the city of Corinth. He said, **"I am afraid as the serpent deceived Eve by his craftiness, that your minds might be led astray from the simplicity and purity of devotion to the Christ."**

Over the last 6 years we have come to understand what it means to embrace the message of "Jesus plus nothing". To embrace this is to embark on a diligent process of removing the man-made add-ons that have been attached to Jesus. When you start out in this process, it is easy to get caught up in the simplicity and purity of devotion to Jesus. At first, it's easy to drop off many of these add-ons. I mean, many of them are so obviously in the way and a distraction from Jesus.

Here's where the myth emerges. I hear it more often than I'd like. I hear people say: "I've never found anything so easy in all my life. It's easy to follow Jesus." This is it! If you feel this way, then I'm not sure you quite "get it" yet. On a certain level, this might be understandable in that you don't have to stuff your mind and life with all of the legalistic add-on stuff. But there is a myth here just the same.

I am returning to the decision I made when Jesus apprehended my life in a fresh way a few years ago. I said then and mean it more today: "I'm trying to do the most difficult thing I've ever done in my life—to follow the teachings and principles of Jesus."

"Jesus plus nothing" is simple and easy to understand, however living this kind of lifestyle is not so simple and easy. This is clearly seen in a few of the interactions with Jesus. It's much easier to just operate your life with a checklist, and then check them off as you do them. "Jesus plus nothing" is not a system of do's and don'ts—a system of beliefs or a checklist. It's a relationship—a day-in-day-out relationship with Jesus.

One of these interactions with Jesus is found in the Gospel of John (John 6): **Jesus answered, "Very truly I tell you, you are looking for me, not because you saw the signs I performed but because you ate the loaves and had your fill. Do not work for food that spoils, but for food that endures to eternal life, which the Son of Man will give you. On him God the Father has placed his seal of approval."**

Then they asked him, "What must we do to do the works God requires?" Jesus answered, "The work of God is this: to believe in the one he has sent."

So they asked him, "What sign then will you give that we may see it and believe you? What will you do? Our ancestors ate the manna in the wilderness; as it is written: 'He gave them bread from heaven to eat.'"

Jesus said to them, "Very truly I tell you, it is not Moses who has given you the bread from heaven, but it is my Father who gives you the true bread from heaven. For the bread of God is the bread that comes down from heaven and gives life to the world." "Sir," they said, "always give us this bread." Then Jesus declared, "I am the bread of life. Whoever comes to me will never go hungry, and whoever believes in me will never be thirsty.

But here is the bread that comes down from heaven, which people may eat and not die. I am the living bread that came down from heaven. Whoever eats of this bread will live forever. This bread is my flesh, which I will give for the life of the world." On hearing it, many of his disciples said, "This is a hard teaching. Who can accept it?"

From this time many of his disciples turned back and no longer followed him. "You do not want to leave too, do you?" Jesus asked the Twelve. Simon Peter answered him, "Lord, to whom shall we go? You have the words of eternal life. We have come to believe and to know that you are the Holy One of God."

Here you have a very difficult time among the many disciples. When

Jesus made Himself out to be the bread of life—the new manna in town, He invited them into a personal, intimate relationship with Him. It's like eating of the bread—taking me into your lives in such a way that you ingest me. Because of this difficult challenge by Jesus to come into a dynamic relationship with Him and learn to trust Him, many left Him.

Where did they go? I think they went back to the simple and easy life of going to Synagogue each week and dropped out of the Jesus movement. It was just too difficult to struggle through cultivating a relationship with Jesus.

It's the same today. The "Jesus plus nothing" lifestyle is not simpler and easier. If you believe that, you are mything out! I am committed to being a stubborn follower of Jesus and this is the most difficult thing I've ever tried to do in my life. The internal struggles are tough, but so worth it. How do you do the works of God? Get caught up into obeying, waiting and trusting Jesus for everything, then you'll have the satisfaction of doing the work of God.

DISCUSSION...

What keeps you from embracing a lifestyle that is simply Jesus?

What is meant by "Jesus plus nothing"?

Do you understand why it is the most difficult thing you'll ever do in your life—to follow the teachings and principles of Jesus? Explain.

MYTH #20
JESUS TAKES A STAND AGAINST SINNERS

This can be a subtle, deceptive myth. It's popular within much of Christianity to "take a stand" against sin and sinners. Therefore Christianity is known for its stands—political stands, values stands, stands against homosexuality, against same-sex marriage, against abortion and on and on and on.

There are three damages here: FIRST—When your emphasis is to "take a stand against" something or someone, you become known for your gloom and doom attitude and turn off those who are looking on.

SECOND—Even though you may have great intentions to fight against corruption, you will find yourself standing against the same people you want to share the good news with. It's very difficult to have it both ways, as we've discussed in an earlier myth.

THIRD—The greatest damage is that by following this myth, you will most certainly miss the example of Jesus and His Good News message. To debunk this myth I want to share a few observations.

FIRST—Jesus didn't take a stand against sinners. There were two kinds of people in the days of Jesus—the religious and the sinners. Jesus didn't seem to have any difficulty with the sinners at all, but His constant struggles and battles were against the religious.

SECOND—Jesus didn't take a stand against sinners; He stood side by side with them.

THIRD—Jesus didn't take a stand against sinners; He even sought them out to hang out with them.

Let's check out a few illustrations of Jesus standing side by side and even hanging out with sinners. When Matthew, a tax-collector, was called by Jesus, there is an interesting scene at dinner in Mark 2: **Once again Jesus went out beside the lake. A large crowd came to him, and he began to teach them. As he walked along, he saw Levi son of Alphaeus sitting at the tax collector's booth. "Follow me," Jesus told him, and Levi got up and followed him.**

While Jesus was having dinner at Levi's house, many tax collectors and sinners were eating with him and his disciples, for there were many who followed him. When the teachers of the law who were Pharisees saw him eating with the sinners and tax collectors, they asked his disciples: "Why does he eat with tax collectors and sinners?" On hearing this, Jesus said to them, "It is not the healthy who need a doctor, but the sick. I have not come to call the righteous, but sinners."

In Matthew 11:19 it is recorded: **The Son of Man came eating and drinking, and they say, 'Here is a glutton and a drunkard, a friend of tax collectors and sinners.'** That's how He was identified with respect to sinners—as their friend.

In Luke 7 Jesus has another interesting encounter with sinners: **When one of the Pharisees invited Jesus to have dinner with him, he went to the Pharisee's house and reclined at the table. A woman in that town who lived a sinful life learned that Jesus was eating at the Pharisee's house, so she came there with an alabaster jar of perfume. As she stood behind him at his feet weeping, she began to wet his feet with her tears. Then she wiped them with her hair, kissed them and poured perfume on them. When the Pharisee who had invited him saw this, he said to himself, "If this man were a prophet, he would know who is touching him and what kind of woman she is—that she is a sinner." Jesus allowing sinners to be near Him and touch Him really stirred up the religious leaders.**

Then in Luke 15: **Now the tax collectors and sinners were all gathering around to hear Jesus. But the Pharisees and the teachers of the law muttered, "This man welcomes sinners and eats with them."** And again Luke records in chapter 19: **All the people saw this and began to mutter, "He has gone to be the guest of a sinner."**

Jesus didn't stand against sinners, so why should we? Jesus identified with them, loved them and sought them out, so why don't we? Jesus went to the sinners instead of inviting them to come to an event He was leading. This is precisely where I believe we have gone wrong for so many years. We seem to think the most effective way to reach out to people in need of God is to invite them to come to us rather than going to them. By the way, the early Jesus movement did not grow through promoting large events and building large facilities, inviting the world to come and join them. The spontaneous expansion of the church of Jesus spread by contagious followers of Jesus touching other individuals and families with the Good News of the love of Jesus.

One more thing is important here. The modern day Jesus movement is spreading spontaneously and massively throughout the world by taking Jesus into the marketplace. The Jesus movement is all about standing with the sinners—the non-religious—hanging out with them in their world. It's not about standing against the sinners and pointing them out, but about standing with them and pointing them to Jesus.

DISCUSSION...

Have you ever fought in a cause that was a good cause, but became more important than Jesus?

Why do you think Jesus put such emphasis in His ministry on sinners and those who just don't have it together?

Why did Jesus seem to be against the religious leaders of His day?

MYTH #21
JESUS' MESSAGE IS SPREAD BEST BY TALKING

This myth has become universal in its impact and yet more and more people understand its limitations. By believing that the best way to spread the Good News message of Jesus is by talking, you are very limited in your perspective and probably not that effective.

We have called this method of talking the Gospel—witnessing. Many classes and seminars have been given to help believers know how to talk more effectively and yet most people carry a lot of guilt because they are unable to get their mouths to work when it comes to witnessing.

The damage here is, at least, fourfold:
FIRST—You limit yourself to getting people to hear your pastor or teacher. Getting people into the church service becomes the most important thing you can do to spread the message of Jesus.

SECOND—You become a preacher. It's been my experience that people don't respond well to you breaking out into preaching. If they wanted to hear you preach, they would ask you to start a church.

THIRD—You become deductive—telling others what and how to believe. This takes away from the heart of the Good News. The Good News message is entirely relational. But if you think talking is the best way to spread the message, you will be spreading a system of beliefs rather than a simple and dynamic relationship with Jesus.

FOURTH—You tend to think in terms of finding out what the best argument is for a given group or flavor of people, so you can approach them more effectively. This focuses you on what your differences are with those who are not your particular flavor and not what you might have in common.

To debunk this myth I want to share only from the words of Jesus as to how to spread His message. The four ways Jesus teaches may not be exhaustive, but they are powerful.

FIRST—Jesus says that your lifestyle will be a light to those who are looking on. **"You are the light of the world. A city on a hill cannot be hidden. Neither do people light a lamp and put it under a bowl. Instead they put it on its stand, and it gives light to everyone in the house. In the same way, let your light shine before others, that they may see your good deeds and glorify your Father in heaven."** (Matthew 5:14-16) NOTE the message of Jesus will be spread through your lifestyle of good works and people will notice in a positive way. Also, note that there is no talking here emphasized.

SECOND—Jesus says that your love for one another will spread His message.

"A new command I give you: Love one another. As I have loved you, so you must love one another. By this everyone will know that you are my disciples, if you love one another." (John 13:34-35) Note there is no talking emphasized here either.

THIRD—Jesus reveals another way that will have a most definite impact in the world that demonstrates the heart of Jesus. **"Then the King will say to those on his right, 'Come, you who are blessed by my Father; take your inheritance, the kingdom prepared for you since the creation of the world. For I was hungry and you gave me something to eat, I was thirsty and you gave me something to drink, I was a stranger and you invited me in, I needed clothes and you clothed me, I was sick and you looked after me, I was in prison and you came to visit me.' "Then the righteous will answer him, 'Lord, when did we see you hungry and feed you, or thirsty and give you something to drink? When did we see you a stranger and invite you in, or needing clothes and clothe you? When did we see you sick or in prison and go to visit you?' "The King will reply, 'Truly I tell you, whatever you did for one of the least of these brothers and sisters of mine, you did for me.'** (Matthew 25) Here being aware of Jesus' heart spreads the sacrificial love message of Jesus and that Jesus can be found in those in need in our world—the hungry, the thirsty, the naked, the stranger, the sick, and those in prison. Jesus also spoke directly to those who didn't notice Jesus in the midst of the needy. **"He will reply, 'Truly I tell you, whatever you did not do for one of the least of these, you did not do for me.'** When we are aware of the poor and needy around us, we are demonstrating the heart of Jesus in our world. Jesus always sought them out and so should we. And when we do, the attractiveness of the sacrificial love of Jesus shines through. Again, there is no talking here.

FOURTH—Jesus sends His twelve disciples out on a mission. Note what He sends them to do: Jesus called his twelve disciples to him and gave them authority to drive out evil spirits and to heal every disease and sickness. As you go, proclaim this message: **'The kingdom of heaven has come near.' Heal the sick, raise the dead, cleanse those who have leprosy, drive out demons**.

Jesus goes on to say that there will be certain divine appointments that they are going to have and doesn't want them to worry about what they will say. He says, **"Be on your guard; you will be handed over to the local councils and be flogged in the synagogues. On my account you will be brought before governors and kings as witnesses to them and to the Gentiles. But when they arrest you, do not worry about what to say or how to say it. At that time you will be given what to say, for it will not be you speaking, but the Spirit of your Father speaking through you."**

FINALLY, Jesus encourages them to say something. He says three things about talking. 1. He will give His disciples authority and power to go spread the message. 2. He gave them the primary theme of their message. It was the message of the presence of the Kingdom. 3. Don't worry about what you will say when you are in a divine appointment, because Jesus promises you that you will be given the appropriate things to say. So, quit talking so much and start embracing Jesus as a lifestyle, learn how to love one another and take on the heart of Jesus for those in need, then He will give you what to say when you need it. St. Francis of Assisi put this myth in perspective with his famous statement: "Preach the Gospel at all times and when necessary use words."

DISCUSSION...

What difficulties have you experienced when it comes to talking about your faith or witnessing?

What kinds of things did Jesus teach that were more effective than talking?

MYTH #22
JESUS SENT PAUL PRIMARILY TO THE GENTILES

This myth is so common and is so easily debunked that it becomes a tester for whether or not we are really paying attention to the words of Jesus as recorded in the Gospel writings. How is it possible to have the words of Jesus clearly written, not requiring any linguistic or cultural interpretation, to be so misunderstood and mis-taught? Yet we are finding these kinds of myths all around us.

The greatest damage comes when those who are freshly searching out the teachings and principles of Jesus discover that the traditional teachings don't match up with what Jesus actually did and said. In fact, there is such an undercurrent of concern within Christianity right now over losing the youth. This has been called the last Christian generation and I think there is great reason for this concern. It's because of teaching and holding to the many man-made traditions and teachings that just cannot be established by a simple reading of the life of Jesus. What's lacking is authenticity. This is why we continue to work our way through the many myths that have developed over the years.

This myth has a couple of dimensions. The first dimension is the traditional division that says Peter was sent to the Jews and Paul was sent to the gentiles. That's even the way I was taught how to divide the book of Acts. Acts 1-8 was about Peter and 9-28 was all about Paul.

Again, we just pass on what we've heard and don't take the time to actually read what really happened. In chapter 9 of Acts Paul is on his way to Damascus and Jesus apprehends him there. Let's look in on it: **As he neared Damascus on his journey, suddenly a light from heaven flashed around him. He fell to the ground and heard a voice say to him, "Saul, Saul, why do you persecute me?" "Who are you, Lord?" Saul asked. "I am Jesus, whom you are persecuting," he replied. "Now get up and go into the city, and you will be told what you must do."**

The men traveling with Saul stood there speechless; they heard the sound but did not see anyone. Saul got up from the ground, but when he opened his eyes he could see nothing. So they led him by the hand into Damascus. For three days he was blind, and did not eat or drink anything.

In Damascus there was a disciple named Ananias. The Lord called to him in a vision, "Ananias!" "Yes, Lord," he answered. The Lord told him, "Go to the house of Judas on Straight Street and ask for a man from Tarsus named Saul, for he is praying. In a vision he has seen a man named Ananias come and place his hands on him to restore his sight." "Lord," Ananias answered, "I have heard many reports about this man and all the harm he has done to your people in Jerusalem. And he has come here with authority from the chief priests to arrest all who call on your name."

But the Lord said to Ananias, "Go! *This man is my chosen instrument to proclaim my name to the Gentiles and their kings and to the people of Israel.* **I will show him how much he must suffer for my name."**

NOTE *who Jesus describes as the focus for Saul's new mission for Him—the gentiles, their kings and the people of Israel.* It is not just to the gentiles; it's wider than that. Also note what His responsibility is to be. Many miss this! Saul is to proclaim or carry the name of Jesus to the gentiles, their kings and the house of Israel. He is not to take a doctrinal system, but the name of Jesus.

The second dimension of this myth is that there was a Jewish man named Saul who became a Christian and his name was changed to Paul. I remember this being taught in Sunday school as a child. Saul, the Jew, became a Christian and now is called Paul, his Christian name. This simply is not true. Paul is called Saul 13 additional times in Acts after the 9th chapter. Saul is his name in Hebrew and he was known as Paul among the Romans and Greeks. There is no Christian conversion of a Jew to Christianity implied here at all.

Think about something with me. As I have spent many days in the *Acts of Jesus* I am seeing Paul in a little different way. In the classic sense of the word, Paul was what we call a Christian today—a follower of the Christ. He was devoted to the Christ—the Messiah, so much so that he was really ticked off with the people of the Way about their views of the Messiah. He was so devoted to the Christ that he was willing to persecute and stop all others who claimed to be followers of the Christ, especially those who disagreed with his view. So here is Paul, a Christian—a follower of the Christ, and as he was acting out his Christian beliefs, Jesus apprehended him on the road to Damascus. I love this! This is what has happened to me. After being educated beyond my intelligence in theology and Bible, Jesus apprehended my life and I hope I never recover from it.

Now, I am a stubborn follower of Jesus to proclaim or bear the name of Jesus in every way I can. Whereas I used to defend Christianity; now I all I want to do is advance the conversation about Jesus. How about you? What are you arguing about or advancing in your relationships?

DISCUSSION...

Have you been operating under the illusion that Paul was sent to the Gentiles? Who was he sent to?

What was it that Jesus told Ananias to tell Paul to do when he came before the people Jesus was sending him to?

Did you grow up believing God changed Saul's name to Paul when he became a "Christian"? Why did this happen do you think?

MYTH #23
CHRIST IS JESUS' LAST NAME

This myth is a simple one. We so often refer to Jesus as JESUS CHRIST that it seems like Christ is Jesus' last name. Well, it isn't. That is a myth—a common misunderstanding. The debunking process is very simple—that is, Christ is Jesus' title. It is best translated as "the Christ" or "the Messiah".

Now in order to work our way through this myth I think it's best to examine the title, CHRIST, and then the name, JESUS. FIRST—The term "Christ" literally means to anoint—to rub or smear a symbolic oil or ointment on someone to establish a person in an official position. In the Hebrew culture there were three major offices among the people of Israel—prophet, priest and king. Each of these official positions were filled with people who were anointed—sort of set apart unto the God of gods. These three offices were quite distinct. The prophet spoke God's words to the people—representing God to man. The priest offered sacrifices, prayers and praises to God on behalf of the people—representing man in the presence of God. The king ruled over the people as God's representative on earth—representing the original dominion of man. Each person who was anointed was functioning as a servant of God.

Although these three anointed positions were distinct and exercised by different people in the Old Testament, they are all three united in the one person of the coming Messiah—the Christ. All three are fulfilled and brought to an ultimate conclusion in the Christ. The Christ—the anointed one—was to be God's servant—the Son of Man.

The threefold misery of men required the threefold offices of God's Messiah. The first is ignorance of what God requires and how man falls short. This requires God's prophet. The second is guilt that occurs due to the shortcomings or sins of the people. This requires God's priest. The third misery of man is the bondage and corruption that results from man attempting to rule over man. This requires God's king to rule over His Kingdom.

Therefore, mankind desperately needs the touch and work of God's Messiah—the Christ. Jesus is born of the Spirit of God, taking on flesh to fill all three official positions of the Christ. Jesus then is able to embrace the title of the Christ. He is best known as Jesus, the Christ. To think Christ is Jesus' last name misses the point of the official positions Jesus fulfilled for mankind.

SECOND—The name of Jesus all by itself without the title is highly significant and most powerful. In order to get this in perspective we must go way back to nearly 3500 years ago when Moses was being sent by God to face the people of Israel. **Moses said to God, "Suppose I go to the Israelites and say to them, 'The God of your fathers has sent me to you,' and they ask me, 'What is his name?' Then what shall I tell them?" God said to Moses, "I AM WHO I AM. This is what you are to say to the Israelites: 'I AM has sent me to you"** (Exodus 3:13-14).

From the beginning God's name was very important. His name is I AM WHO I AM. This personal name of God means that God exists and always has existed. It is spelled in the Hebrew language by four letters without any vowels. It is YHWH. Some ancient rabbis have described the name of God as like taking a breath. It is Yah-weh. And every breath you take is like saying His name. His name is revered so highly by the Jewish people that they wouldn't even pronounce it. Instead they would use the word for "lord" in its place. Even today, most Jews will not spell out the word, God. They usually write it with a hyphen, G-d.

When we come to the time of Jesus, there is a lot of emphasis placed upon the name of Jesus. In the first few verses of John it says, **In the beginning was the Word, and the Word was with God, and the Word was God. He was with God in the beginning. Through him all things were made; without him nothing was made that has been made. In him was life, and that life was the light of all people. The Word became flesh and made his dwelling among us. We have seen his glory, the glory of the one and only.**

Later in John Jesus says, **"And I, when I am lifted up from the earth,**

will draw all people to myself." What is it about this Jesus that is so attractive? Well, in Acts 4:12 it says, **Salvation is found in no one else, for there is no other name given under heaven by which we must be saved. There is something about that name**.

Remember when the Lord spoke to Ananias about what he was to tell Paul, whom Jesus had just apprehended on the road to Damascus. He said, **"Go! This man is my chosen instrument to proclaim my name to the Gentiles and their kings and to the people of Israel."**

When Jesus prayed to the Father in John 17, He makes an interesting reference about the name of God, **"Holy Father, protect them by the power of your name, the name you gave me, so that they may be one as we are one. While I was with them, I protected them and kept them safe by that name you gave me."**

So what is the name of God that was given to Jesus? It is Jesus or "*Yeshua*" in the Hebrew. NOTE what this means. It is a combination of YE, short for Yahweh, and SHUA which means saves. So, the name is YAHWEH SAVES-*Yeshua*. It's a combination of the name of God given to Moses and the Messianic name given to God in the flesh—Jesus—God saves!

Even more specific is that Jesus makes several claims to being the I AM. When Jesus announced to His disciples He would be leaving, Thomas said, **"Lord, we don't know where you are going, so how can we know the way?" Jesus answered, "I am the way and the truth and the life. No one comes to the Father except through me."**

To think Christ is Jesus' last name not only misses the point of the official positions Jesus fulfilled, but also misses the person of Jesus. Jesus, the Christ—Jesus, the name above all names, and the Christ, the highest position God ever established. To accept this myth is to diminish Jesus the Christ in such a way that He cannot have His way in your life. Always remember, it's Jesus, the Christ.

DISCUSSION...

What is the problem with thinking Christ was Jesus' last name?

Which name has more power—Jesus or Christ?

Why is the name of Jesus so easy to leave out of our materials and conversations?

MYTH #24
SATAN DOESN'T BELIEVE JESUS IS THE SON OF GOD

This is a very different myth, but well worth tracking. There was a great challenge in the beginning to spread the Good News of Jesus to the Jewish and non-Jewish cultures. Jesus was not from a traditional school. Everyone was astonished at the authority with which Jesus taught. He didn't quote anyone. The authority, authenticity and attractive perspective on old truths and traditions were awesome and revolutionary. It was so different from what they had been taught.

Endless questioning and debating followed Jesus everywhere. Everyone had an opinion on Jesus' identity. Even the disciples had a sense of doubt and timidity about what they really thought about this Jesus. They were a work in progress, for sure.

But in the midst of all of this questioning and discussion about who this new Rabbi Jesus was, there is a group who already and always knew the true identity of Jesus. This group is so unlikely. That's why I call it a myth. The groups are energized and serve as emissaries of Satan. Satan does believe Jesus is the Son of God.

The only ones who greet Jesus as He enters a village and already know He is the Son of God are the demons. In Mark 3:10-12 it says, **For he had healed many, so that those with diseases were pushing forward to touch him. Whenever the evil spirits saw him, they fell down before him and cried out, "You are the Son of God."**

Luke records another scene where Jesus is met by the demons and they say, **"Go away! What do you want with us, Jesus of Nazareth? Have you come to destroy us? I know who you are—the Holy One of God!"**

In Mark 5 is another occurrence: **When he saw Jesus from a distance,**

he ran and fell on his knees in front of him. He shouted at the top of his voice, "What do you want with me, Jesus, Son of the Most High God? In God's name don't torture me!" For Jesus had said to him, "Come out of this man, you evil spirit!"

In Acts 19 Luke records an interesting interaction with the demons: **Some Jews who went around driving out evil spirits tried to invoke the name of the Lord Jesus over those who were demonized. They would say, "In the name of Jesus, whom Paul preaches, I command you to come out." Seven sons of Sceva, a Jewish chief priest, were doing this. One day the evil spirit answered them, "Jesus I know and I know about Paul, but who are you?" Then the man who had the evil spirit jumped on them and overpowered them all. He gave them such a beating that they ran out of the house naked and bleeding. When the Jews and Greeks living in Ephesus knew this, they were all seized with fear and the name of the Lord Jesus was held in high honor.**

NOTE the claim by the demons, "Jesus I know", and they did. They knew who Jesus was. They were clear on His identity. Also, note that the people who witnessed and/or heard of this interaction with the demons were made to have great fear and the name of Jesus was held in high honor.

It's been my experience that when you see Jesus through the eyes of Satan, you see Jesus and His power more clearly. Satan knows and believes Jesus is the Holy One of God—the Son of God. The more I have seen the face of evil the more I understand the power of the name of Jesus. Greater is Jesus in you than Satan's demons all around you. Don't get fascinated and distracted by the activities of demons and evil today. Focus on Jesus as the Holy One—the Son of God. Satan and his demons believe this and know it to be true. Do you believe this? This is one time I'd suggest that you agree with Satan.

DISCUSSION...

Who was the only group in every village that knew exactly who Jesus was, even before being introduced?

Why do you think this is?

What kind of attitude did these demons have toward Jesus? Why?

MYTH #25
JESUS REQUIRES THAT ALL PRAY THE "SINNER'S PRAYER"

Since the 1950's most of evangelical Christianity has nearly totally embraced a theological concept that has come to be known as the "Sinner's Prayer." There are so many varieties of what this prayer is, but basically it is a prayer event where a person acknowledges he/she is a sinner and needs the Savior. Many believe Jesus requires that everyone must pray such a prayer in order to have salvation. That simply is not true. It's a myth!

One of the first questions that must be asked is, "Where is the sinner's prayer in Scripture?" It's just not there. There are two that have become most popular. One is the scene in Luke 18:9-14. It's where Jesus tells a parable where two men are observed praying—one a sinner and the other a religious Pharisee. Let's look at it: **And He also told this parable to some people who trusted in themselves that they were righteous, and viewed others with contempt: "Two men went up into the temple to pray, one a Pharisee and the other a tax collector. "The Pharisee stood and was praying this to himself: 'God, I thank You that I am not like other people: swindlers, unjust, adulterers, or even like this tax collector. 'I fast twice a week; I pay tithes of all that I get.' "But the tax collector, standing some distance away, was even unwilling to lift up his eyes to heaven, but was beating his breast, saying, 'God, be merciful to me, the sinner!' "I tell you, this man went to his house justified rather than the other; for everyone who exalts himself will be humbled, but he who humbles himself will be exalted."**

This is a great comparison between a humble sinner and a prideful Pharisee, but it is not a universal special prayer that somehow must be prayed for salvation. Jesus just doesn't mean it for that reason.

The second common passage used to illustrate what a sinner's prayer might look like is in Revelation 3:20: **'Behold, I stand at the door and knock; if anyone hears My voice and opens the door, I will come in to him and will dine with him, and he with Me.'** Although this has a great imagery to it, the context for this verse has to do with those who are already believers, but they are not fellowshipping with Jesus—maybe not walking with Him as He would like.

The damage of believing there is some sort of magical happening or prayer that one prays that will automatically bring about salvation is to miss what salvation is all about. You might call it "accepting Christ" or "meeting Christ" or "receiving Jesus as your personal Savior", but this just isn't what Jesus taught.

You might site Paul's encounter with Jesus on the road to Damascus as the norm, but that experience is hardly the norm. It's very unique. Or, you might site the 3000 who were added to the early fellowship in one day in response to Peter's message on the Day of Pentecost. That's recorded in Acts 2:41: **So then, those who had received his word were baptized; and that day there were added about three thousand souls**.

But when you closely examine what is said about the 3000, you will discover a phrase that may give us the key to what really is going on. Later in that passage Luke says, **They were praising God and having favor with all the people. And the Lord was adding to their number day by day those who were being saved**. NOTE "those who were being saved". "Being saved" is used elsewhere and this offers a way to debunk the myth that there is required some eventful prayer—the sinner's prayer mentality—that will bring a person into salvation.

Let's take the 3000 and analyze what happened to them. FIRST—They received the message of Peter about Jesus. They agreed with the Good News message of Jesus.

SECOND—They were baptized to identify themselves as followers of Jesus. This was a Jewish tradition—to be baptized into whomever you are following. They were baptized into Moses, they were baptized with John's baptism and now here they are being baptized as followers of Jesus.

THIRD—The Lord added them to the fellowship of Jesus to follow Him together. They practiced discussing the teachings of the apostles, praying, eating and enjoying fellowship together. No one was pushing anyone into participating in this Jesus fellowship. This was a God-thing!

FOURTH—They were BEING SAVED. They weren't saved, but being saved. The way I see it this action of responding to Peter's message and being baptized was the initial step of being saved. The act of believing enough to respond in this way was the beginning of the process of being saved.

There are several illustrations of this initial step today. There is the altar call where people go down front in response at the end of a service. There is throwing a stick in a campfire and expressing one's desire to follow Jesus. There is the method of the "I Believe!" part of a service where a person stands to his feet and says out loud, "I believe!" All of these methods of response don't bring you salvation in and of themselves, but they are each an initial step in salvation of BEING SAVED. The problem comes when you are expecting that this initial response is the entire closed-out event and you are in!

FIFTH—Note there is no prayer in this response of the 3000 at all—not the sinner's prayer or any other kind of prayer.

There was a time that I tried to count how many times I had gone forward or responded to God in a public way, looking for a life-changing experience. I was looking for a climactic event where I finally meant it and actually got it all from God. I counted 42 times, but none of them delivered what I was looking for. It's because I was looking for the wrong thing. I was caught up in what our church's traditions and teachings were. I just didn't understand what Jesus wanted me to do.

So, there just isn't a clear "sinner's prayer" or climactic spiritual event in the teachings of Jesus that indicates any kind of requirement. Instead, Jesus simplifies what the prayer or the action must be for anyone who is leaning into following Him. Jesus said in Matthew 11:28-30: **"Come to Me, all who are weary and heavy-laden, and I will give you rest.**

"Take My yoke upon you and learn from Me, for I am gentle and humble in heart, and YOU WILL FIND REST FOR YOUR SOULS. For My yoke is easy and My burden is light."

NOTE Jesus is all about each of us simply "coming to Him"; it's a relational matter with Jesus. This is why His continual requirement is clearly "Come to Me!" or "Follow Me!"

DISCUSSION...

What's been your experience with the use of the "sinner's prayer"?

What is the problem with using this prayer as a general method of outreach?

What is the most important thing to do for anyone who is searching out what salvation and spiritual life is all about?

MYTH #26
TO JESUS SALVATION IS ALL ABOUT HEAVEN

The emphasis upon salvation throughout the years tends to over focus on salvation as the channel or gateway to heaven. This has become an overriding theme in Christianity and yet is a myth. Salvation is so much more than a gateway to heaven or eternal life.

In the Old Testament Scriptures the concept of Shalom is a primary theme. Shalom is where people experience a peaceful and satisfying relationship with every aspect of life. Shalom encompasses the idea of peace, wellbeing, prosperity, and the experience of God's blessings. Everywhere in the Old Testament, peace and prosperity are seen as God's reward to those whose ways are pleasing to Him. In Proverbs 16:7 it says: **"When a man's ways are pleasing to the Lord, he makes even his enemies live at peace with him."** And in Psalm 128:1–2 it says: **"Blessed are all who fear the Lord, who walk in his ways. You will eat the fruit of your labor; blessings and prosperity will be yours."** Where "salvation" or "saved" is used in the Old Testament, it is in a "quite concrete" sense that "covers more than spiritual blessings," such as deliverance from earthly enemies, wellbeing and "the effect of God's goodness on his people". This sense of an all-embracing salvation is continued in the New Testament, even though the more spiritual aspect of forgiveness of sin receives a stronger emphasis today.

Jesus speaks of a wider sense of what salvation means. In Luke 7:50, Jesus says to the "sinful woman" regarding forgiveness of her sins, **"Your faith has saved you"**, and in Mark 10:52 He uses the same Greek word for the blind man to imply restoration of sight. In Mark 5:28, He uses "saved" with a double meaning when he told the woman who had been suffering from bleeding, **"Daughter, your faith has healed you, go in peace and be freed from your suffering."** The word "healed" there is the word for "salvation". So, physical healing and spiritual salvation are found in the same term. Jesus didn't separate the physical from the spiritual.

Several years ago I delved into the term "salvation" and found several dimensions of its meaning and this revolutionized my thinking. Let me list them out:

1) **Salvation means to make wide**—This is a freedom from being stuck, from distress and the ability to pursue one's own objectives and unique purpose in life.

2) **Salvation means God will come through on your behalf**—I love this one. Wait and see the mighty deeds of God. God uses divine intervention in the midst of a crisis. However, He uses divine appointments in the continual process of life.

3) **Salvation means safety and security**—to maintain life unafraid of numerous dangers!

4) **Salvation means healing**—This is emotional and physical well-being—wholeness. This is the essence of the Hebrew word Shalom.

5) **Salvation means constant redemption**—God is true and loyal to His covenant with man and always seeks man's restoration.

6) **Salvation destroys the purposes of evil forces**—You can count on it. No matter how much evil throws at you, God is there to protect.

8) **Salvation means God's love in action**—It flows from His love as God is courting and wooing us back to Him.

9) **Salvation means the active presence of God among His people**—This is one of my favorite parts of salvation. God is present right here, right now, working in and through each one of us.

Jesus never thought of salvation in terms of heaven only. There was so much more to it in His mind and teachings. You see, when you embrace this myth you diminish the fullness of salvation for yourself. With this myth you tend to wait around for the "sweet bye-and-bye" and ignore what's happening now on earth. To hang out with Jesus and walk with

Him, you must be present right here, showing up for the divine appointments He continually sets up for you every day. This is what it means
to really love Jesus—to love God with all your heart, strength and mind
and to love your neighbor as yourself.

There is a funny story that sums up this myth. A very religious man approached another man on the street corner and asked, "Do you want to
go to heaven?" The man quickly replied, "No!" The religious man was
surprised at this answer and said, "I thought everybody wanted to go to
heaven when they die." The man replied, "Oh, I thought you were getting up a group to go right now!" That's the experience of salvation right
here in the present.

Psalm 62:1-2 **Truly my soul finds rest in God; my salvation comes
from him. Truly he is my rock and my salvation; he is my fortress,
I will never be shaken.** Psalm 37:39 **The salvation of the righteous
comes from the LORD; he is their stronghold in time of trouble.
Psalm 40:16 But may all who seek you rejoice and be glad in you;
may those who long for your saving help always say, "The LORD
is great!"**

Only a god who can bring salvation to me down here right now is worthy of worship! Everything else is just pie-in-the-sky, wishful thinking.
Jesus, the Savior, is greater than all other gods and is worthy of your
praise and worship, because of His salvation.

DISCUSSION...

**Why do you think we have made going to heaven such a major focus
in our spiritual thinking and communication?**

**Can you name additional definitions of what salvation means other
than going to heaven?**

What do these do for you?

MYTH #27
THE FINISHED WORK OF JESUS WAS TO DIE

I remember going to special services on Good Friday each year as a kid and the primary theme was the seven words of Jesus on the cross. One of these sayings of Jesus was "It is finished." If you were to survey most Christians today and ask them what was it that was the finished work of Jesus or what did Jesus come to accomplish, you will receive the same answer most of the time. The finished work of Jesus was to die on the cross for the sins of the world. Jesus did come to die and He mentioned this a few times with His disciples, but they just didn't get it or didn't want to get it.

As important as the death of Jesus was, it is a myth that this is why Jesus came. I say this with great backing from Jesus Himself. You see, it's important for us to get back to the teachings and principles of Jesus. His teachings and principles are primary in our understanding of the truth of Jesus. It is true that when Jesus said these words, it marked the finished work of Christ on the cross. He had finished the sacrifice that was required for the redemption of the world.

However, a few days before Jesus died on the cross, He revealed what His finished work actually was—the reason why He was sent to earth. So, what did Jesus say was the work he came to complete? When Jesus prayed to the Father, He prayed for Himself, for His disciples and for us today. This is really the Lord's Prayer. The "Our Father Who art in heaven" prayer is better viewed as the disciples' prayer, when He was teaching the disciples to pray.

So, what was it that Jesus came to do? What is the work He came to complete? The finished work of Jesus is more than what we normally think. It's within these words of Jesus' prayer in John 17 that we can find the true revolutionary nature of what Jesus came to do and what He expects from us as disciples. Jesus said that He finished the work the Father sent Him to do: **I have brought you glory on earth by finishing** the work you gave me to do. Notice what Jesus says is the finished work He came to do.

"I have manifested Your name to the men whom You gave Me out of the world; they were Yours and You gave them to Me, and they have kept Your word. "Now they have come to know that everything You have given Me is from You; *for the words which You gave Me I have given to them; and they received them* and truly understood that I came forth from You, and they believed that You sent Me.

"But now I come to You; and these things I speak in the world so that they may have My joy made full in themselves. I have given them Your word."

Jesus came into this world to invest His life in a few men and now He sends us out to do the same. **"As You sent Me into the world, I also have sent them into the world. "For their sakes I sanctify Myself, that they themselves also may be sanctified in truth. "I do not ask on behalf of these alone, but for those also who believe in Me through their word; that they may all be one; even as You, Father, are in Me and I in You, that they also may be in Us, so that the world may believe that You sent Me. "The glory which You have given Me I have given to them, that they may be one, just as We are one; I in them and You in Me, that they may be perfected in unity, so that the world may know that You sent Me, and loved them, even as You have loved Me...and I have made Your name known to them, and will make it known, so that the love with which You loved Me may be in them, and I in them."**

Jesus invested in a few—all the ones God brought to Him. I believe this is the finished work of Jesus. He invested in the 12 and lost one of these, so He gave Himself to eleven men. Now if this strategy was good enough for Jesus, then don't you think it's the best strategy for you and me as well?

I spent most of my life preparing and training to invest my life to move the masses toward Jesus. Now I know this was the wrong strategy. Just as Jesus met and gave healing to one person at a time, so we are to do the same. Let me ask you something. What are you doing with the people God has brought to you? Are you investing your life and teachings in these few? Jesus saw this work as the most important work ever. Don't you think we can take a clue from Jesus and do the same?

DISCUSSION...

What was the finished work of Jesus? What was He sent to do?

Since He has sent His followers to do the same, what is it that you are to do with your life?

Who are the people the Father has sent your way?

MYTH #28
JESUS IS OPPOSED TO ALLAH

Before 9/11 hit the USA, I was not much of a student of Islam. I had read the Qur'an, but without much interest or understanding. After 9/11, we were all shocked into a crash course on terrorism and Islam. Sermons, articles, books and Christian talk shows spewed out the Christian talking points on "Islam" and most everyone bought into them without much personal research.

One of the biggest and most common of the "talking points" was in the analysis of the Muslim name for their God—Allah. What was taught and bought was that Allah was an ancient Moon god and therefore had no connection with the God of the Bible. The battle lines were drawn again between Christian and Muslim. Certainly Jesus must be opposed to using the term Allah and we must separate ourselves from it and Allah's followers. But, I have come to understand this as a myth—a deadly misunderstanding.

Congressman Mark Siljander in his groundbreaking book, *A Deadly Misunderstanding*, says, "This is one of the most painful misunderstandings among Christians. Nearly all Christians universally feel that Allah is **not** the same God as the God of the Hebrews, or Abraham, Isaac, Jacob and Ishmael." Televangelists, pastors and radio hosts continued to spread the misunderstanding throughout the Christian world.

You may be able to demonstrate that the name Allah was originally the name given for a moon god, but there is no Moslem today who believes he is praying or submitting to the moon god, but to the God of gods— Allah. But once this is said, someone inevitably points out that the Muslim world is actually calling on the moon god unknowingly.

This doesn't hold water at all. The people of Israel used the name of a Canaanite god "El"—a god that was worshipped as a bull deity (hence the idea of forming a golden calf)—and they came to call their God of gods "Elohim" — a plural form of El to denote the Godhead. In the Aramaic language of Jesus' day, the language Jesus used, Elohim would have been spoken as "Alah". And before Mohammed was born, Arab-speaking followers of Jesus would have used this same word — Alah.

The same thing can be said for the English word we use, "god". The Latin for God is "dios", which was originally used by pagans. Siljander notes: "'God' is derived from a proto-Germanic pagan word for a water god, water spirit, or idol (pronounced 'gut')." Or, take the Latin word for god "dios", which became "theos". This has a heathen Greek origin, taken from the same root for the god Zeus. So, when you use the name "God", do you really mean or are you calling up a "water god"? Or, when you use the word "theos" where we get our word theology — the study of god, are you calling up Zeus? Absolutely not! We have taken these terms and infused them with the meaning of the God of gods.

Siljander points out: "For over 500 years before the Prophet Moham-med, Arab Christians and even some Jews in the Arabian Peninsula used the Arabic word 'Allah' for God. How about the 10-12 millions of Christian Arabs who use Allah every day as their Arabic word for God? Do they remotely consider that they are praying to a Moon -god? Not at all! What of the five million Assyrian and Chaldean Christians who pray to 'Alaha,' being the same derivative of Allah?"

The Aramaic word for God is "Elahh" or "Alaha" and the Arabic word for God is "Elahh" or "Allah". If you saw Mel Gibson's movie, The Passion of the Christ, you know that it was filmed in Aramaic. Jesus spoke Aramaic. Therefore, when Jesus spoke of God, He would have used "Alaha" and this is simply the Arabic version of "Allah". When Jesus said, "Blessed are the pure in heart for they shall see God, He used "Alaha" or in the Arabic Bible, "Allah".

So, is Jesus opposed to Allah? No way! That's a bad myth. On the contrary, Jesus came as the fleshed-out form of Allah to the Muslims, of Alaha to the Assyrians and Chaldeans, of Elohim to the Jews, of God to the Germanic Christians and to every other cultural name given to the God of gods. You see, Jesus trumps everything! JESUS is the name above all names and someday everyone will come to acknowledge Him. Jesus, simply and wonderfully and irresistibly Jesus!

DISCUSSION...

Why is it that Christians are so naturally opposed to Allah being a legitimate name for the God of gods?

What implications come from the fact that Jesus called the God of gods "Allah" as He spoke in Aramaic?

How will this change your attitude toward the Muslims?

MYTH #29
JESUS WANTS YOU TO BE HEALTHY,
WEALTHY & SUCCESSFUL

There is something inside most of us that believes that if we are walking with God, our God will make us more successful. And, if I am faithful to my God, then my God will keep me in His healing hands and keep me healthy. Certainly the God of gods is able to do all of the above and more.

This has become a damaging myth to so many. The first area of damage is to use God as you might use a genie. This is thinking that God works for you. Have you ever heard someone say, "I tried God out and He didn't work for me." Well, if you think in this way, then you have it all backwards. The Lord doesn't work for you; you are to work for Him.

The second area of damage in embracing this myth has been repeatedly applied by Christian radio and TV personalities. It is the presumption that if you give your money to God's work, then God will pay your bills. One preacher specifically asks his viewers to tally up the total of their bills and send a check for that amount to his ministry. And, believing this myth, many people actually follow through and send their checks.

The third area of damage for those who embrace this myth that God wants you to be healthy, wealthy and successful is to come to believe that they are having troubles because their faith is too weak. If Jesus wants me to be healthy, wealthy and successful and I am not any of these, then I must feel spiritually inadequate—like a spiritual midget, at best.

To debunk this myth I want to offer three observations. FIRST—Jesus speaks of suffering as a norm for those who are His disciples. Even when He gave Paul's mission through Ananias, Jesus said, **"and I will show him what he must suffer."**

SECOND—In one of the earliest books written after the Gospels—the book of Hebrews—there is a major chapter that lists out the Hall of Faith, demonstrating how God works in response to man's faith and faithfulness. But after so many successes of faith are listed, the writer of this book turns the corner a bit. The results are not always positive when a person exercises his faith in God. In some cases, people were sawn in two, stoned, lost their children by death, lived in caves and holes in the ground and their wardrobe was made of animal skins. Now that doesn't sound like healthy, wealthy and successful to me.

THIRD—How much does Jesus want from those who follow Him? There are basically four dimensions of your life as you relate to the Lord—time, treasure, talent and touch.

1 Time—How much of your time does Jesus want from you? You might revert to the principle of the Sabbath and say He wants one-seventh of your time—one day a week. However, as you examine what Jesus requires, I think you'll come to a different conclusion. Jesus wants 100% of your time. You are to be a follower of Jesus and one who practices His Kingdom all of the time—not part time, but full time.
2. Treasure—How much of your money and stuff does Jesus want from you? You might revert to the principle of tithing and say what He wants is 10%. However, as you examine the teachings of Jesus, I think you will discover that He wants everything you have—100%. You own nothing. He owns everything you have and all that you are. You are to be the manager of your money and stuff for Jesus and His Kingdom.
3. Talent—How much of your talent does Jesus want from you? Since He gave it to you and empowers you to use it, I think you'll find that He wants it all—100%.
4. Touch—How much of your touch—your relationship with people—does Jesus want? Every time you come into relationship with anyone, you are to love that person and every time you find a person in need, you are to do what you can to meet those needs—hunger, thirst, clothing, and shelter. He wants your 100% attention.

You see, Jesus doesn't want you to be healthy, wealthy and successful as much as He wants YOU. Nothing else really matters to Jesus, but knowing and walking with you. Jesus doesn't even want to hold first place in your life. First place implies that there are many other places that are ranked in importance and can easily crowd out whatever is in first place. You may be healthy or ill, wealthy or poor, a success or a failure, but Jesus wants to be at the center of it all. Jesus doesn't want first place; He wants to be the center of everything you are and all that you do. So, why not turn it over—100%.

DISCUSSION...

What does Jesus want from you with respect to your health and successfulness?

What are the four dimensions of your life that Jesus wants?

Which is the easiest for you? The most difficult?

MYTH #30
JESUS TEACHES A LOT ABOUT HELL

I remember as a kid noting that Jesus talked more about "hell" than He did heaven. That made quite an impression on me, that Jesus felt He must teach so much about it. But a closer look at what Jesus taught will demonstrate that He didn't teach about "hell" at all! It's a myth—a well-preserved and emotional one, at that. There is a lake of fire mentioned only in the book of Revelation, but Jesus didn't teach about it.

I've always known through my study of the Greek New Testament that the translators of the Bible, beginning with the King James made a universal decision to translate many words as hell. I never really understood the problem with it until I heard Rob Bell, a teacher of the Bible in a most relevant way, speak on the subject of hell in the middle of a series he was doing. The series was called "God Wants To Save Christians" and he was saying that God wants to save Christians from missing the point in many areas.

In the New Testament there are a few words that are translated "hell" by many of the early Bible translators, but these translations are being slowly changed. In one case, hell is translated from the word, Tartarus (II Peter 2:4). Tartarus is a designation for the dwelling place of the fallen angels or the underworld. In the second, hell is translated from the word, Hades, which is the equivalent of Sheol in the Hebrew language. These are found in Matthew 16:18, Revelation 1:18; 6:8; 20:13; 20:14. This is also translated as "death", "the grave", and "the pit". None of these words means hell in the classic sense of the word as it has become known and feared today.

The third word translated as hell is Gehenna. Gehenna does not mean hell either, yet this is the word Jesus frequently used. It is used eight times by Jesus (twelve, if you count the times a different writer repeated the same story). In Matthew 5:22, Jesus says: **"But I say to you that everyone who is angry with his brother shall be guilty before** the court; and whoever says to his brother, 'You good-for-nothing,' shall be guilty before the supreme court; and whoever says, 'You fool,' shall be guilty enough to go into the fiery hell."

In Matthew 5:29-30, Jesus says: **"If your right eye makes you stumble, tear it out and throw it from you; for it is better for you to lose one of the parts of your body, than for your whole body to be thrown into hell. If your right hand makes you stumble, cut it off and throw it from you; for it is better for you to lose one of the parts of your body, than for your whole body to go into hell."**

In Matthew 10:28, Jesus says: **"Do not fear those who kill the body but are unable to kill the soul; but rather fear Him who is able to destroy both soul and body in hell."**

Then in His blasting of the religious leadership in Matthew 23, Jesus says: **"Woe to you, scribes and Pharisees, hypocrites, because you travel around on sea and land to make one proselyte; and when he becomes one, you make him twice as much a son of hell as yourselves."** And later in that chapter, He says: **"You serpents, you brood of vipers, how will you escape the sentence of hell?"**

Here's the question that must be asked in order to understand what Jesus was teaching: What did His audience think He was referring to, when He used the word, "Gehenna"? Gehenna is literally "the Valley of Hinnom"—Jerusalem's city dump, where children were sacrificed to Molech. Judean Kings Ahaz and Manasseh engaged in idolatrous worship there, which included the making of human sacrifices by fire to Baal. Later, King Josiah pronounced this horrible, fiery, garbage pit accursed, because of the horrendous human sacrifices performed there. The prophet Jeremiah cursed the place and predicted that it would become a place of death and corruption.

When Jesus used this term—Gehenna, those who were listening certainly didn't think to themselves that He was talking about a future destination called hell. Instead, they believed He was referring to that wretched, accursed, useless place—the fiery garbage pit—always burning. He was saying to the angry, the lustful, the religious leaders who were leading others astray and those who are fearful of the wrong things: "You deserve to be thrown into the pit of destruction, because you are useless and worthless because of these actions." "You are worthy of the Valley of Hinnom; you are worthy of Gehenna."

Jesus was not talking about a future location, but a place of worthlessness and uselessness right here, right now. He wasn't speaking of a lake of fire, but a place defiled and was used as the city's garbage dump; a place of rotting flesh, maggots, stench and fire. This may be one of the most powerful Christian rumors ever and should be a strong reminder to pay attention to what Jesus is really saying. This is certainly one of those times when the traditions and commands of men have made the commands and teachings of God ineffective and misleading. God wants to save Christians, alright; He wants to save them from missing the point!

DISCUSSION...

Why do you think the translators so consistently used the term "hell" for the word, Gehenna?

In your own words, what did Jesus meet by Gehenna?

With this new understanding, what does it mean to your many discussions with people?

MYTH #31
MISSING THE MESSAGE OF JESUS BEGAN WITH THE ORGANIZED CHURCH

This is a common myth among those of us who are so fed up with the damages of organized Christianity. It's so easy to identify the culprit in leading us away from Jesus' message as the artificial Christianization of Emperor Constantine, the atrocious Crusades, the corruption of the Roman Catholic Church or the divisiveness of the more than 35,000 sects within Christianity since the Protestant Reformation. However, to think that missing the message of Jesus began with these organizational travesties is to buy into a major myth and miss the point of what it is that goes wrong when the message of Jesus is ignored.

No, the organized Church is not where missing the message of Jesus began. It began from the very beginning with the early disciples of Jesus. There seems to be a natural tendency, no matter how much we have seen and heard, to become distracted away from the simplicity of Jesus plus nothing.

I want to walk you through one of my favorite passages that illustrate this truth unmistakably and you will also see yourself as we take a quick glimpse of what happened to the disciples. In the 9th chapter of Luke Jesus does a most unusual thing. He sends His disciples out, empowered to drive out demons, to cure diseases, to proclaim the message of the Kingdom and to heal the sick. What makes this most incredible is that Jesus sends out these disciples who aren't really believers yet nor do they yet believe Jesus is the Son of God. So they went out into many villages and performed their mission as prescribed by Jesus. Think of it! They are brand new followers of Jesus and they have already been sent on a mission to perform incredible miracles among the people! What an experience this must have been!

Next Jesus took them with Him to a nearby fishing village in Galilee where great crowds followed them. After speaking to the crowds about the Kingdom of God and healing many of them, Jesus knew they needed to eat something so He fed over 5000 people with five loaves of bread and two fish. Jesus performed this spectacular miracle by using the disciples to distribute the food to the masses of people. What a thrill that must have been for these disciples!

About eight days after telling His disciples that His Messianic mission included the necessity of dying, Jesus then takes Peter, John and James with Him up on a mountain to pray. While praying Jesus revealed His glory and brilliance as the visible presence of God right in front of them—the Shekinah glory. Moses and Elijah supernaturally appear with them and then the voice of God pronounces Jesus as the Son of God. Again, this must have been an amazing experience for these three disciples.

When they came down from the mountain, a large crowd met them. A man was concerned for his son who was afflicted with seizures and convulsions and complained to Jesus that the other nine disciples were unable to heal him. Jesus moves into gear and heals this man's son right away. Everyone, including the disciples was amazed at this sight!

These disciples have just been sent out to perform miracles in the villages, participated in the feeding of the 5000, three of them saw Jesus in all His glory, and they all saw Jesus heal this desperate little boy. What a ride! What a miraculous adventure watching Jesus do His thing and actually working alongside Him.

NOW, note what happens in the next three scenes with the disciples. They royally miss the preeminence of Jesus and His message. FIRST— An argument breaks out among the disciples: **An argument started among the disciples as to which of them would be the greatest. Jesus, knowing their thoughts, took a little child and had him stand beside him. Then he said to them, "Whoever welcomes this little child in my name welcomes me; and whoever welcomes me welcomes the one who sent me. For whoever is least among you all is the greatest."**

What's this all about? After all of this demonstration that Jesus is the preeminent One, they have already missed the point. Jesus is the point, not them and their comparative greatness!

SECOND—The disciples become jealous over seeing another person doing things in the name of Jesus: **"Master," said John, "we saw someone driving out demons in your name and we tried to stop him, because he is not one of us." "Do not stop him," Jesus said, "for whoever is not against you is for you."** Now, the disciples are caught up in comparison again. This time the problem is that there is a person doing things in the name of Jesus. Now note this! John says the problem with this person is that **he is not one of us.** Do you get it? This guy who is doing terrific things in the name of Jesus just doesn't match up, because he is not a member of their little group. Ever heard or seen that attitude? Again, they are missing the preeminence of Jesus. Their little group has become more important than Jesus, Himself.

THIRD—There is a problem with the response of the Samaritans: **As the time approached for him to be taken up to heaven, Jesus resolutely set out for Jerusalem. And he sent messengers on ahead, who went into a Samaritan village to get things ready for him; but the people there did not welcome him, because he was heading for Jerusalem. When the disciples James and John saw this, they asked, "Lord, do you want us to call fire down from heaven to destroy them?"** But Jesus turned and rebuked them. Now, it's getting worse! The disciples are now so miffed at the Samaritan's response that they are actually suggesting that they must be destroyed. Note, it's more serious than this. They aren't asking Jesus to call down fire from heaven; they are thinking that they might have the power in themselves to call the fire down to destroy the Samaritans—"Lord, do you want us to call fire down from heaven to destroy them?" Are you kidding me? These guys have not only missed the preeminence of Jesus; they are taking on a little personal preeminence for themselves.

Missing the message of Jesus did not begin in the organized Church; that's a myth. It began with the earliest disciples of Jesus; even before the Jesus movement was officially launched! They missed it within a period of a few days in which they experienced the most miraculous adventure anyone could have ever imagined.

Who's the greatest? This guy is not one of us! Let's destroy these Samaritans who aren't receptive to our message! None of these responses by the disciples is on-message with what they have experienced in their walk with Jesus. They completely missed the point. JESUS IS THE POINT OF IT ALL! Do you see it that way or are you missing the point in your life?

DISCUSSION...

Why do you think Jesus empowered these early disciples to actually heal and participate in the feeding of the 5000?

Take each of the three responses by the disciples at the end of Luke 9 and define what's going on in your words. Can you identify with what they were feeling? Have you thought the same thing?

MYTH #32
JESUS TAUGHT WHEN HE IS COMING BACK

There are two areas within the world of biblical teachings that can get people so fired up that they become distracted away from the heart of the matter. One is the subject of demons or evil spirits. The other is the area of prophecy. There are so many varied teachings on the 2nd coming of Jesus.

What's most interesting is that each position held is taught in such a way so as to make you think this is THE WAY to understand it. "Our way is right and yours is wrong." And the division continues to widen between well-meaning followers of Jesus. Divisiveness is the first area of damage in embracing this myth. When you think Jesus has clearly taught when He will return and you are the one who knows when that time will be, you will prove to be divisive.

Each prophecy teacher dogmatically stands on his teachings and against the teachings of others. There is certainly nothing wrong with disagreeing over when Jesus is coming back, but to reject or separate yourself from other followers of Jesus because of your disagreement is sick and wrong.

Over the years I have made fun of the differing positions regarding when Jesus will show up again—specifically in the rapture—the time that believers will be caught up to meet Jesus in the air. Some believe in the pre-tribulation rapture theory that Jesus will show up before the final seven-year tribulation period. Some believe in the mid-tribulation rapture theory that Jesus will show up in the middle of the seven-year tribulation—three and one-half years into the final tribulation period. Then others believe in the post-tribulation rapture theory that Jesus will show up at the end of the tribulation period.

Many years ago I came to an unshakeable position on this. I am pre-trib until the tribulation starts. And if Jesus hasn't shown up by then, I will move quickly to a mid-trib position. And if Jesus doesn't show up by mid-night, three and one-half years into the tribulation, then I will swiftly move into a post-tribulation rapture theory position. And, I will not be shaken from this position. I call it the pan-trib position, meaning everything is going to pan out in the end anyway, no matter your position on the subject.

Distraction away from the primary message of the Good News of Jesus is the second area of damage in embracing this myth. When you think Jesus has clearly taught when He will return and you know when that time is, it is easy to become distracted away from cultivating a personal relationship with Jesus.

If you believe Jesus taught WHEN He is coming back and you think you know when that will be, you will be divisive and will add to the distractions away from the person of Jesus.

Jesus does speak a lot about coming back, but you will be hard-pressed to nail down the WHEN. Oh, I know most of the prophetic teaching positions that are popular today. I've even been a major proponent of prophetic teachings over the years. As I look back on that period of my life, I was so distracted away from my walk with Jesus and others, because of my focus on the latest and greatest fulfilled prophecies.

Now, since Jesus apprehended my life a few years ago, I have been less focused on WHEN Jesus is to return and am spending lots of my time and energy in getting to know WHO Jesus is. I began to be haunted by the words of Jesus in Matthew 24 and 25. Let's check a few of these out. Jesus says: "For just as the lightning comes from the east and flashes even to the west, so will the coming of the Son of Man be." He also says: "Therefore be on the alert, for you do not know which day your Lord is coming." And again Jesus says: "For this reason you also must be ready; for the Son of Man is coming at an hour when you do not think He will."

What haunts me are the words of Jesus in Matthew 24:36: "But of that day and hour no one knows, not even the angels of heaven, nor the Son, but the Father alone." Now, if Jesus means what He says here, then maybe the WHEN is not the important thing. If Jesus doesn't know the WHEN, then what makes any bible teacher think that he or she could possibly know it?

Don't get caught up in prophecy in such a way that you are divided from other brothers and sisters and are distracted away from learning to walk with and trust Jesus in your life right here right now. Don't focus on the WHEN. Jesus didn't teach it and you can't know it. Focus on the WHO—ON JESUS HIMSELF. That's how you can be on the alert or be ready. Nothing else really matters in comparison!

DISCUSSION...

What is the potential problem with having the end-time prophecies all figured out?

Why do you think this is such a popular Christian teaching and theme?

Where does it place the focus—in the future or in the now? And the problem is?